THE FOOD AND COOKING OF MILAN AND BOLOGNA

THE FOOD AND COOKING OF
MILAN
AND BOLOGNA

CLASSIC DISHES FROM THE NORTH-WEST OF ITALY

VALENTINA HARRIS

PHOTOGRAPHY BY MARTIN BRIGDALE

aquamarine

This edition is published by Aquamarine,
an imprint of Anness Publishing Ltd,
Blaby Road, Wigston,
Leicestershire LE18 4SE

Email: info@anness.com

Web: www.aquamarinebooks.com;
www.annesspublishing.com

If you like the images in this book and would like to investigate using them for publishing, promotions or advertising, please visit our website www.practicalpictures.com for more information.

Publisher: Joanna Lorenz
Project Editor: Kate Eddison
Copy Editors: Catherine Best and Jan Cutler
Designer: Simon Daley
Photographer: Martin Brigdale
Food Stylist: Valentina Harris
Prop Stylist: Martin Brigdale
Illustrator: David Cook
Indexer: Diana Lecore
Production Controller: Wendy Lawson

PUBLISHER'S NOTE
Although the advice and information in this book are believed to be accurate and true at the time of going to press, neither the authors nor the publisher can accept any legal responsibility or liability for any errors or omissions that may have been made nor for any inaccuracies nor for any loss, harm or injury that comes about from following instructions or advice in this book.

NOTES
Bracketed terms are intended for American readers.
For all recipes, quantities are given in both metric and imperial measures and, where appropriate, in standard cups and spoons. Follow one set of measures, but not a mixture, because they are not interchangeable.

- Standard spoon and cup measures are level. 1 tsp = 5ml, 1 tbsp = 15ml, 1 cup = 250ml/8fl oz. Australian standard tablespoons are 20ml. Australian readers should use 3 tsp in place of 1 tbsp for measuring small quantities.
- American pints are 16fl oz/2 cups. American readers should use 20fl oz/2.5 cups in place of 1 pint when measuring liquids.
- Electric oven temperatures in this book are for conventional ovens. When using a fan oven, the temperature will probably need to be reduced by about 10–20°C/20–40°F. Since ovens vary, you should check with your manufacturer's instruction book for guidance.
- The nutritional analysis given for each recipe is calculated per portion (i.e. serving or item), unless otherwise stated. If the recipe gives a range, such as Serves 4–6, then the nutritional analysis will be for the smaller portion size, i.e. 6 servings.
- Measurements for sodium do not include salt added to taste.
- Medium (US large) eggs are used unless otherwise stated.

Front cover shows Trenette with Pesto in the Genoese Style – for recipe, see page 43

A CIP catalogue record for this book is available from the British Library.

ETHICAL TRADING POLICY
At Anness Publishing we believe that business should be conducted in an ethical and ecologically sustainable way, with respect for the environment and a proper regard to the replacement of the natural resources we employ.

As a publisher, we use a lot of wood pulp to make high-quality paper for printing, and that wood commonly comes from spruce trees. We are therefore currently growing more than 750,000 trees in three Scottish forest plantations: Berrymoss (130 hectares/320 acres), West Touxhill (125 hectares/305 acres) and Deveron Forest (75 hectares/185 acres). The forests we manage contain more than 3.5 times the number of trees employed each year in making paper for the books we manufacture.

Because of this ongoing ecological investment programme, you, as our customer, can have the pleasure and reassurance of knowing that a tree is being cultivated on your behalf to naturally replace the materials used to make the book you are holding.

Our forestry programme is run in accordance with the UK Woodland Assurance Scheme (UKWAS) and will be certified by the internationally recognized Forest Stewardship Council (FSC). The FSC is a non-government organization dedicated to promoting responsible management of the world's forests. Certification ensures forests are managed in an environmentally sustainable and socially responsible way. For further information about this scheme, go to www.annesspublishing.com/trees

CONTENTS

AN ALPINE LANDSCAPE

In the north-west of Italy lie the five regions of Lombardy, Piedmont, Liguria, Emilia-Romagna and the tiny Aosta Valley. The contrasts between these five close neighbours are astonishing. The modern metropolitan centres of Milan, Turin and Bologna, the thriving independent port of Genoa, the ancient cities of Mantua and Cremona and the remote mountain villages of the Aosta Valley all lie within close proximity of each other, nestling between the Apennines and the Alps. It is the landscape created by this fascinating and rugged backdrop that binds these regions together. The mountainous exterior surrounds the fertile basin of the river Po, where many wonderful ingredients are grown, which form the basis of the area's culinary heritage.

THE MIGHTY RIVER PO

From its source in the mountains close to the French border to its estuary on the Adriatic coast, the Po is the lifeline of the north-west, gathering in all the water that flows from both the Apennines and the Alps. The river is prone to flooding and is heavily polluted, so fresh water for agriculture and drinking comes from thousands of wells dotted throughout this low-lying landscape. These natural springs and the fertile silt deposited by the river over centuries have led to the Po basin becoming the centre of Italian industry, with an almost continuous urban development stretching 550km/342 miles from Turin to Trieste. Fields of precious crops fill the basin, as do large-scale food factories, which make this area one of Italy's most important food producers.

THRIVING LOMBARDY

Lombardy lies in the centre of northern Italy, bordering Switzerland. One-sixth of Italy's population lives here, many in the regional capital, Milan. The summers are humid, and the winters can be cold, foggy and rainy. The great lakes, Garda, Maggiore, Lugano and Como, which, apart from Garda, lie in the high mountains on the border with Switzerland, are favourite tourist destinations. The micro-climate around the lakes allows the cultivation of typically Mediterranean produce such as olives and citrus fruit, even in these high regions. South of the Alps lie gentle hills, dotted with small, fertile plateaux where sheep and cows can graze.

Lower down, modern agriculture takes over. This area is Italy's major farming centre, with field upon field of wheat, rice and other grains, interspersed with protected parks of astonishing natural beauty.

MOUNTAINS AND PLAINS OF PIEDMONT

The name of this region is a contraction of the Italian phrase 'ai piedi del monte', meaning 'at the foot of the mountain'. The area is surrounded on three sides by the Alps. From the highest peaks the land slopes down gently to hilly areas, with an

BELOW *Liguria and Emilia-Romagna enjoy beautiful coastlines on opposite sides of Italy.*

BELOW RIGHT *The north-west of Italy is framed by mountains to the north, west and south, with a fertile river basin running through the centre.*

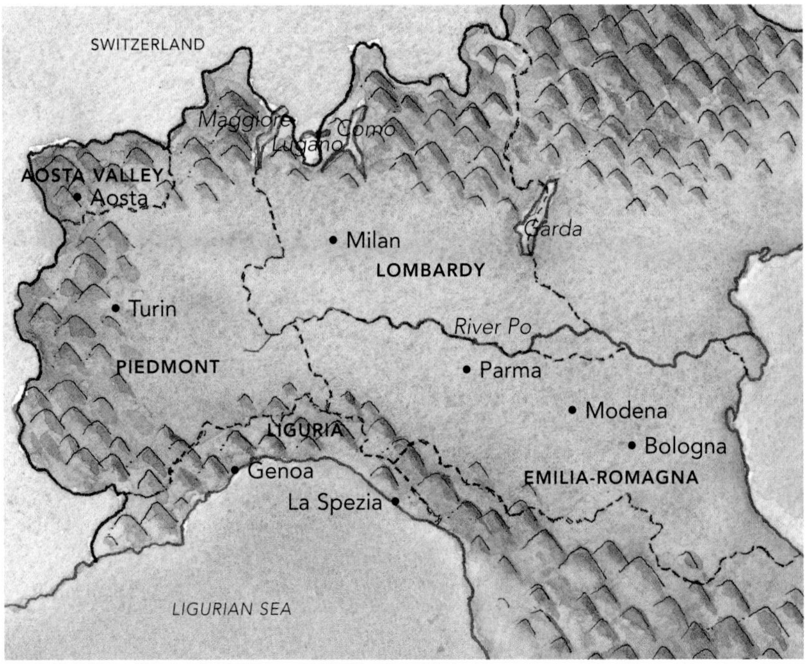

occasional sudden drop where the mountains meet the plains. Farming is a major industry in the low-lying areas beneath the mountain slopes, with vast fields of rice and maize as well as some of the best vineyards in Italy, which produce top-class wines. The regional capital, Turin, is one of the biggest and busiest cities in Italy.

SPECTACULAR LIGURIA

Liguria is renowned for its stunning beaches, picturesque towns and utterly delicious food. It winds around the coast in a narrow band, and has a temperate climate due to the warm waters of the Ligurian Sea, as well as the natural barrier that is created by the mountains, protecting Liguria from the cold northerly winds. The climate is mild all year round, and rainfall can be abundant, giving the region a lovely green landscape. The vast majority of the population lives and works in the thin strip of habitable land around the coast, and this is where Liguria's specialist farmers produce their top-quality olive oil and flowers, which are exported all around Europe.

LOCAL LANGUAGES

The people in the north-western regions bordering France and Switzerland speak many dialects, some far removed from the 'classical' Italian of Rome and Florence. Examples include: Western and Eastern Lombard, Piedmontese, Emilian and Franco-Provençal. These languages are proudly maintained and are in daily use, particularly in the high, mountainous areas of the Aosta Valley.

HARD-WORKING EMILIA-ROMAGNA

The lower plains of the rivers Po and Adige form the region of Emilia-Romagna (actually two distinct regions of Italy combined into one). The landscape has been farmed from Etruscan and Roman times; since the Middle Ages the local people have been almost entirely focused on agriculture as a business, with organized trading opportunities provided by monastic orders, feudal lords and free communes. The co-operative farming system is still in working order today.

The produce of Emilia-Romagna is extremely varied and ranges from fruits and vegetables of countless kinds to grains and livestock, not to mention grapes, which are used to produce many splendid wines from the region.

THE REMOTE AOSTA VALLEY

Italy's tiniest region, Aosta Valley, is tucked away into the highest corner of the Alps, north of Piedmont. It borders both France and Switzerland, neighbours who have always influenced the cooking of the largely French-speaking population. It is now an autonomous region, meaning that it controls its own finances and planning. Farmers mainly concentrate on raising dairy cattle in the high Alpine pastures, producing milk for the wonderful cheeses made here, as well as growing grapes to make some top-quality wines.

In recent years much has been made of the tourism opportunities in this picturesque area, with winter sports, such as skiing, and summer walking holidays proving very popular. The breathtaking landscape, fabulously clear air and excellent food culture make it a tremendously sought-after destination.

ABOVE LEFT *Portofino, on the glorious Ligurian coast, has an array of pretty, coloured houses that line the waterfront.*

ABOVE *Lake Como, in Lombardy, is a tourist hot spot, boasting a benign climate much of the year, and dazzling views of the majestic Alps.*

A HISTORY OF POWER

The rich heritage of the northern part of Italy can be seen everywhere in these five regions. Empires rose and fell, trading links were forged and battles were fought over this land. The valleys are so fertile and the hills and mountains so spectacular that it is no surprise to find that many tribes have settled here. Meanwhile, traders from the north passed through these regions on their way farther south, bringing exciting new foodstuffs and recipes with them, and Ligurian ports, such as Genoa, were gateways into Italy for exotic spices, fruits and vegetables. Roman ruins dot the landscape of northern Italy, Medieval towns nestle in the hills and beautiful Renaissance architecture embellishes the cities.

BELOW *Milan's elegant Gothic cathedral occupies a central position in the city, dominating the skyline.*

LOMBARDY – FINANCIAL POWERHOUSE

The city of Milan, centre of the Lombardy region, was founded by Celtic tribes who extended their rule all the way to the Adriatic Sea. From 194BC, Roman culture overwhelmed the Celtic civilization, and in the years that followed, Lombardy became one of the richest areas of Italy, with the construction of good roads and the swift development of agriculture and trade. Taking full advantage of the flourishing economy, Lombardy continued to trade and make deals until it became the financial centre of the whole of Europe. The word 'Lombard' in Renaissance England came to mean any merchant or banker from northern Italy.

From the Renaissance to the Napoleonic era, this thriving region was fought over with gusto by its neighbours, France and Austria, but finally, in 1859, Lombardy was officially reunited with the rest of Italy and confirmed its status as the powerhouse of Italian finance. Its busy regional capital, Milan, is the centre of its economy, as well as its food culture, being home to some of the most characteristic Lombard dishes: for example the delicious saffron-flavoured risotto, which takes a little time to cook but is well worth the effort. The general rule in this hectic city is that making money must never take precedence over a good dinner!

PIEDMONT – ANCIENT REPUBLIC

Like Lombardy, Piedmont was vulnerable to attack from France and Austria. It was inhabited in early historic times by Celtic-Ligurian tribes and later conquered by the Romans.

In the Middle Ages and through the Renaissance, some Piedmontese areas remained independent, such as Asti (now famed for its sparkling wine), Alessandria, Saluzzo and Montferrat. At the Congress of Vienna in 1814–15, the Kingdom of Piedmont-Sardinia also took charge of the Republic of Genoa (now in Liguria) as a barrier against French invasion.

Piedmont was the initial springboard for Italy's unification in 1859–61, and Turin briefly became the capital of Italy. Today Piedmont manages to preserve ancient traditions amid the fast pace of modern life, including its food cultures. It is famous for its 'Slow Food' movement, which symbolizes this trend.

LIGURIA – SEAFARING REGION

The isolated coastline of Liguria has been open to marauding Saracens, Normans or pirates arriving by sea since the 5th century BC, when the Ligurian people first arrived to give the region its name.

By the Middle Ages the port of Genoa dominated all of Liguria and had become a powerful maritime republic, in many ways stronger than its rivals in Pisa and Venice. Eventually Genoa faltered and lost most of its power, and Liguria was annexed by Napoleon and given to the House of Savoy. This loss of independence inspired patriots such as Mazzini and Garibaldi to start the Italian Risorgimento, which in turn led to the establishment of the modern nation of Italy.

In the first years of the 20th century the region's economic growth was remarkable, and specialized industries such as olive and herb farming flourished all along the coast. During the Second World War, Liguria experienced two years of privation under occupation by German troops. However, when Allied troops reached Genoa towards the end of the war they were surprised to find Italian partisans welcoming them. In a successful insurrection, they had freed the city, and Genoa was awarded a gold medal for military valour.

AOSTA VALLEY – PROUDLY INDEPENDENT

In common with the other northern regions, the Aosta Valley was overrun by tribes from both north and south, including early Celts and Ligurians. The Romans arrived around 25BC and improved the links with other regions by building roads and passes through the mountains. However, the Aosta Valley always tried to preserve its independence and traditional culinary customs, which means it is quite different from the southern parts of Italy. Its cuisine focuses on local ingredients such as the many delicious cow's milk cheeses made by cattle farmers in the high mountains. The Aosta Valley joined the Kingdom of Italy in 1861, but has retained its independent status as an autonomous region.

EMILIA-ROMAGNA – CENTRE OF TRADE

The name Emilia-Romagna has its history in the Roman legacy of this area. The region was named after the Aemilian Way, a Roman highway built at the height of the Roman empire. During the Middle Ages, trading activities, politics, culture and religion flourished in the region's monasteries and in the University of Bologna, which is the oldest university in Europe.

In the 16th century, most of the small dukedoms became part of the Papal States, but the territories of Parma, Piacenza and Modena remained independent until Emilia-Romagna became part of the Italian kingdom in 1859, one of the first regions to commit to the new regime. Emilia-Romagna covers most of the Po valley, reaching from west to east, which has to led to great wealth in terms of agriculture and industry, as well as a fine gastronomic tradition.

ABOVE *Fénis Castle in the Aosta Valley is a fine example of the splendid medieval architecture that remains in the region.*

BELOW LEFT *Genoa harbour, pictured here in 1870, has long been a thriving, bustling port where new ingredients and food ideas entered Italy.*

BELOW *Students today still study at the grand Bologna University, which, founded in 1088, is the oldest university in Europe and the oldest continually operating university in the world.*

A CLASSIC CUISINE

The complicated history of northern Italy, as well as its proximity to cooler European countries, means that the food is quite different from the cuisine of the south. Instead of consuming pasta at every meal, the inhabitants tend to vary it with substantial amounts of rice and polenta. The foggy, damp plains of the Po valley are ideal places to grow rice, maize and buckwheat, rather than the durum wheat that makes the best dried pasta. (With that said, Emilia-Romagna is the famous home of delectable fresh egg pasta, which is made in all sorts of shapes.) A multitude of other world-famous products hail from this region, including balsamic vinegar from Modena, and Parma ham and Parmesan cheese from Parma.

THE COOKING OF LOMBARDY AND MILAN

Lombardy has acted as a pathway for many different tribes to pass through the Alps, some of whom stayed long enough to leave their mark on the local cuisine. Common elements link all of Lombardy's gastronomy. Generous use of butter is the main hallmark of Milanese and Lombard cooking, as is the general preference for rice or polenta over pasta. Meat, especially veal, is considered the king of the dinner table.

Rice is generally transformed into risotto with tender spring asparagus or freshwater shrimps, turned golden by the addition of saffron, and scented with herbs such as rosemary or sage. Cream is frequently on hand to make rich and sumptuous sauces to dress hearty pasta dishes such as ravioli filled with sausage meat (bulk sausage), potatoes, Swiss chard and herbs.

A popular dish for hot summer days is vitello tonnato, a cold dish of poached veal in a sauce of tuna, mayonnaise and capers. When the weather is cooler, Lombard cooks excel at making costolette alla Milanese (breaded and butter-fried veal chops, rather like Austrian Wiener Schnitzel); bollito misto, where various cuts of beef, pork, poultry, offal and veal are cooked together in a rich broth; or càsoeûla, a stew of pig trotters (feet) and ears, sausage and cabbage, which is typically

BELOW *These flooded rice fields in Piedmont provide excellent rice for making rich risottos.*

accompanied by steaming hot polenta. In this region polenta is made not only of maize but also of buckwheat flour, for example in the popular dish polenta taragna, served with lots of melting cheese.

Desserts include countless crumbly, buttery or crisp biscuits, of which the famous Amaretti di Saronno, almond macaroons, is the most addictive.

CULINARY DELIGHTS OF PIEDMONT

Gastronomy is an everyday passion in Piedmont. The inhabitants are fiercely proud of having at their fingertips many of the world's finest ingredients, such as red wines that rival the greatest that France can offer, and a fantastic range of cheeses and other dairy products, not to mention the luxury of white truffles and award-winning chocolate.

Piedmont's cuisine, like that of its neighbour Lombardy, is rich, with white sauces predominating over red tomato-based ones. They are extremely proud of their exquisite pastry-making tradition and careful attention to detail, which are known and respected throughout Italy. Although pasta in Piedmont is delicious, silky, soft and usually handmade, rice and polenta tend to be more prevalent. Garlic appears mainly in the salty bagna caoda, a savoury 'warm bath' in which vegetables are dipped, which is one of the region's flagship dishes. The idea is that everybody at the table dips chopped vegetables such as carrots, fennel, peppers and Piedmont cardoons into a mouthwatering bowl of warm olive oil, garlic, cream, butter and anchovies.

Another vital part of the Piedmontese food scene is precious white truffles. Rare and expensive, they have a unique flavour, which is celebrated throughout Italy. Their scent is delicate, but pungent and powerful at the same time. Unlike the more common black truffles, white truffles are served only raw, finely grated in beautifully veined shavings that fall like rain over a bed of risotto, or with tajarin, the Piedmontese version of tagliatelle, made with an outrageously rich, eggy dough.

Piedmont grows the world's most sought-after hazelnuts, Tonda Gentile delle Langhe. Experts pay a premium for these because of their subtle flavour. Once blended with silky chocolate, hazelnuts become Nutella, the addictive spread born in Piedmont only 40 years ago. The city of Turin can rightfully claim to have perfected the art of chocolate in Italy. Many cafés and artisan chocolate stores throughout Piedmont offer their own versions of chocolate specialities such as gianduiotti. These stores reflect the recipes and techniques passed down through local families since the 1600s.

It is no accident that the movement known as Slow Food, aimed at promoting traditional cuisine, was born, and still has its internationally powerful base, in Piedmont.

ABOVE LEFT *White truffles are sought out with dogs in the countryside around the town of Alba, in the hills of Piedmont.*

ABOVE *The Langhe area of Piedmont is awash with vineyard-covered rolling hills, where fabulous wines are produced.*

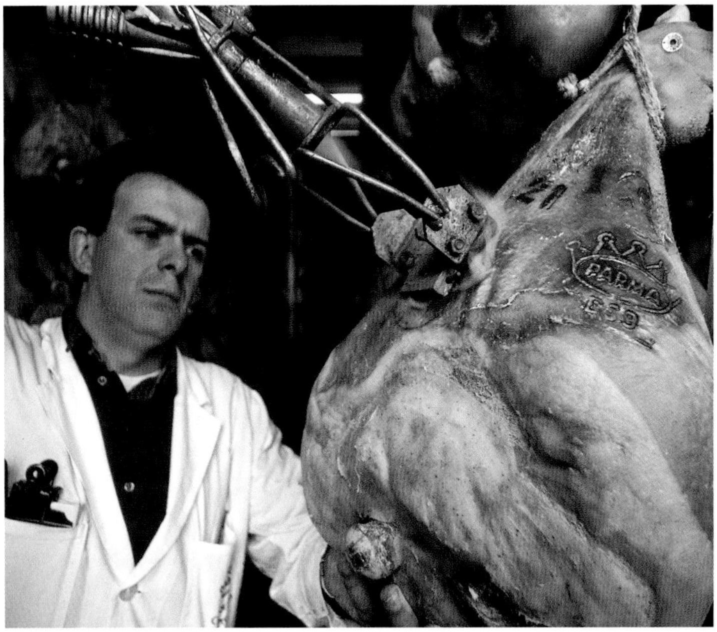

ABOVE *Parma ham, or prosciutto di Parma, is branded with the seal of quality in a factory in Langhirano in the province of Parma.*

ABOVE RIGHT *Parmesan cheese, or Parmigiano Reggiano, is aged in huge storage facilities, where it is monitored by inspectors.*

FRESH TASTES OF LIGURIA

It would be natural to presume that the local cuisine of coastal Liguria would be characterized by fish dishes, plus all the spices, tomatoes and other ingredients first brought to Genoa by traders in the 15th and 16th centuries, yet these are missing from the traditional repertoire. This is because it was not the Ligurian bankers or spice merchants who shaped the local menu, but the sailors of its maritime fleet. The food on board ship was restricted to ingredients that would keep indefinitely, along with fish caught on the journey. When the sailors returned to Genoa, they certainly didn't want to eat more fish. Instead, they craved fruit and vegetables, and herbs such as fresh basil. It is the historic and commercial tradition of Genoa as a major port, along with the pleasant and temperate climate, that has created the region's unique gastronomy, harmonizing the products of the sea, the vegetable garden and the woods.

The cuisine's most notable feature is the use of aromatic herbs, including bay leaves, marjoram and, most importantly, basil. Basil and Liguria are inextricably linked due to the famous sauce pesto, which originated in Genoa. The Genoese have a special passion for basil, and most people grow a pot of this fragrant herb on a sunny windowsill. Some say that the best basil grows only around Genoa, where cool winds from the mountains meet salty sea breezes, giving the basil its distinctive aroma. Undeniably, the basil in Genoa makes its pesto totally unique.

Among other specialities are farinata (a thin pancake made from chickpea flour) and the famous focaccia alla Genovese (a flat bread loaf). Both of these are served by the hundreds of local bakeries, and are consumed as snacks at any time of day, a sort of Italian fast food made with a few natural ingredients: flour, olive oil, salt and water.

Last but not least come the products of the green wooded hills tucked away behind the coastline: chestnuts, mushrooms and truffles, as well as small berries, such as strawberries, whortleberries and raspberries, which are used in a medley of tasty desserts and cakes.

RICH FOOD OF EMILIA-ROMAGNA

The city of Bologna is famous throughout the world for its superb cuisine. Perhaps less well known is the fact that it lies at the heart of Emilia-Romagna, a region celebrated throughout Italy for the range and quality of its ingredients and dishes. From the Adriatic coast to the inland plains and river valleys, the whole area is blessed with excellent products and a wonderful culinary heritage. Now one of the richest areas of Europe, Emilia-Romagna has developed a strong economy based on the building of cars and motorcycles. Agriculture, however, is still a part of the economy. Crops, including cereals, potatoes, maize, tomatoes and onions grow well here, along with many varieties of fruit and grapes that are used in the production of wine. Cattle and pig breeding are also highly developed, and farm co-operatives are hugely successful here.

Emilia-Romagna is the region that gives us exquisite fresh egg pasta in a multitude of shapes, such as tagliatelle, tortellini, garganelli and lasagne. It is also the birthplace of balsamic vinegar, Parma ham, Parmesan cheese, mortadella and a wealth of other cured meats. With this abundance of rich food from the surrounding towns and countryside, it is no wonder that Bologna has aquired the nickname Bologna la Grassa, meaning 'Bologna the fat one'.

THE CUISINE OF THE AOSTA VALLEY

People from the Aosta Valley favour a robust cuisine that is based on cheese, meat, rye bread, potatoes, polenta, gnocchi, risotto and soups. Cows grazing on the lofty Alpine meadows provide fine butter and many excellent cheeses, such as Toma, Robiola and, above all, Fontina, which features in many a local recipe. Perhaps the classic cheese dish from this region is fondua, which is similar to Piedmont's fonduta or a Swiss fondue, made with milk, egg yolks and a luxurious helping of Fontina cheese. Another fantastic local cheese is Fromadzo, a firm cow's milk cheese (sometimes with the addition of ewe's milk) that has been made in the valley since the 15th century. Cheese is also added to polenta, risotto and thick soups, whose ingredients range beyond the usual vegetables, meat, rice and potatoes to include earthy mushrooms, chestnuts and almonds.

Aostans make good use of the freshwater trout that abounds in the mountain streams, and have developed plenty of recipes for this fish. Local game, such as partridge, grouse, hare and venison, is also put to use in a wonderful medley of regional specialities. The local pork products are justly famous, including a prosciutto called jambon de bosses, spicy blood sausages called boudins, and the local salame, which is preserved in pork fat. A strange local curiosity is tetouns, which is made of a cow's udder, salt-cured with herbs, then cooked, pressed and sliced fine like ham.

The Alpine climate in the Aosta Valley lends a fresh flavour to berries and fruit, especially apples and pears, which are poached in good-quality, local red wine to make a really tasty dessert. This region is also noted for fragrant mountain honey, almond biscuits (tegole) and butter crisps known as torcetti.

Meals often conclude with the passing of the grolla, a roughly carved wooden pot containing caffé alla valdostana (coffee with red wine, grappa and lemon peel), sipped from numerous spouts in a truly friendly fashion.

BELOW LEFT *Fresh egg pasta is made by hand in Piacenza, Emilia-Romagna.*

BELOW *Fontina cheese has been made in the Aosta Valley for many centuries.*

FESTIVALS AND CELEBRATIONS

As in other regions of Italy, there is an abundance of small local festivals in the north-west of the country, focusing on local produce when it is coming into season and at its peak of freshness. During these festivals, the cooks demonstrate huge inventiveness in using the products in a medley of fabulous recipes. Religious festivals also give an opportunity for cooks to show off their expertise, with a particular focus on feasts and special local foods at Christmas, such as Milanese panettone, soft almond macaroons and chocolate treats from Piedmont. At Easter, too, there are plenty of local delicacies to be found, such as the lovely soft Easter cake, colomba Pasquale (Easter dove), which is made in the city of Pavia.

FOOD FESTIVALS OF MILAN AND LOMBARDY

The celebration known as Sagra dell'Asparago (Asparagus Feast), which dates back to 1940, is one of the region's main gastronomic events. For four days, the town of Cantello offers asparagus tasting, and local restaurants create a range of special asparagus-based dishes.

In June and September, the Pizzoccheri Festival takes place in Teglio. Pizzoccheri is a pasta shape that looks a little like tagliatelle and is made of buckwheat. It is usually cooked with vegetables and served in broth, topped with butter and cheese.

SARTIRANA LOMELLINA FROG FESTIVAL

The most unusual food festival in Lombardy has to be the Frog Festival at Sartirana Lomellina in September, where delicacies such as rice with frog liver are served.

DELIGHTS OF PIEDMONT

One of the most famous festivals in Piedmont is the Truffle Festival of Alba, celebrated in October and November. This event has been running for more

BELOW *The truffle festival, which takes place in Alba, Piedmont, each autumn is celebrated with a medieval procession.*

than 75 years and draws chefs from around the world. During the festival, the wholesale truffle market opens to the public so people can inspect, and even buy, the delicious white truffles.

The Raschera and Brus Cheese Festival is held at Frabosa Soprana in August. Raschera cheese has an ivory colour and a fine, delicate flavour, which becomes quite pungent when it is left to mature. Brus is a fermented cheese made from both cow's and sheep's milk, with a very strong flavour, and is particularly sought after by gourmets.

The Pumpkin Festival in Piozzo in October each year features more than 120 types of pumpkin, in many shapes and sizes, which are displayed on stalls and wagons throughout the town. Visitors to Piozzo can sample both traditional and modern pumpkin-based dishes in every restaurant.

CULINARY FEASTS OF LIGURIA

The Biscette Festival at Solva di Alassio in March celebrates this typical cake from the Loanese area, made with hazelnuts, flour and sugar, bound together with orange flower water and then fried in olive oil. It is shaped to resemble a snake.

In June, nursery owners display and sell their plants and herbs – especially delicate Ligurian basil – in the streets of the town of Andora. The town of Savignone holds an annual pesto festival using this fragrant local basil. Later in the summer, there is a wonderful celebration of red garlic in Vessalico. This rare vegetable is limited in production to only 3,000 plaits of garlic, each with 24 heads, per year.

The Trenette Festival (trenette are flat, thin ribbons of pasta) is held in August in Loano, where a wonderful assortment of local dishes are served, displaying Ligurian food at its most authentic.

FORGOTTEN FRUITS IN EMILIA-ROMAGNA

An unusual plant known as rampion is celebrated at Borghi on the first Sunday after Easter. Rampion is found growing wild in the fields. Its leaves are edible; they have a pleasant, slightly sweet taste and are often used in salads or boiled and served with vinegar.

The Tortellino Festival (Sagra del Tortellino Tipico) is held annually in Reno Centese, in the province of Ferrara, at the end of June. Here, the keen gourmet can eat tortellini stuffed with everything from truffles to wild herbs, dressed with ragù, melted butter or cream, and also watch the experts make them. This little pasta parcel is supposed to resemble the belly button of Venus, the most beautiful goddess.

Garlic is the king of the Garlic Festival at Voghiera in July, where it is celebrated with garlic-based foods and dishes, garlic tastings, and many traditional activities and games.

At the aptly named Forgotten Fruits Festival at Casola Valsenio in October, it is possible to taste the flavours of exotic and neglected fruits from the area, such as cornelian cherries, vulpine pears, Neapolitan medlars, and many others.

FESTIVALS OF THE AOSTA VALLEY

At the end of June, the little town of Avise dedicates itself entirely to a splendid festival known as La Fiocca, entirely devoted to whipped cream – ideal for those with a sweet tooth. After this, in the second week of July, at Saint-Rhémy-en-Bosses, there is an annual festival in celebration of the local ham, the jambon de Bosses. The French names of both the ham and the town give an indication of how close this region is to the French/Swiss border.

ABOVE LEFT *The Frog Festival at Sartirana Lomellina sees some rather unusual foods served each September.*

ABOVE *Christmas markets surround Milan cathedral every year during the festive season.*

CLASSIC INGREDIENTS

Tradition is the hallmark of the northern Italian regions. Despite the international style of Milan and the busy industrial life of many northern cities, such as Turin and Bologna, local delicacies and their recipes are fiercely guarded. Nowadays, these specialities often have a Protected Designation of Origin (PDO), certified from the European Union as well as an Italian Denominazione di Origine Controllata (DOC) certification to ensure that they are made only with the best local ingredients in the correct manner. These include many types of cheese, cured meat and wine, for example, prosciutto di Parma, Parmegiano Reggiano, Gorgonzola, Fontina, Barolo wine and balsamic vinegar from Modena.

DAIRY PRODUCTS

There are many wonderful varieties of cheese produced in the pleasant countryside of northern Italy. Perhaps the best known is the marvellous strong-tasting Parmigiano Reggiano (Parmesan) cheese, which is made in the Emilia-Romagna region. It takes over 9 litres/15¾ pints of milk to make 450g/1lb of this delicacy, and then it must be matured for a minimum of 12 months. The name is trademarked and there are very strict rules and criteria that each individual cheese must meet before it can be sold as Parmigiano Reggiano. It is used in cooking and is delicious sprinkled on soups, salads and many pasta dishes.

Other lesser-known cheeses also form part of the ancient traditions of northern Italy. Taleggio is named after a valley in the province of Bergamo, and is produced throughout Lombardy. This soft, creamy cow's milk cheese was traditionally ripened in underground caves; today, it is matured in climate-controlled cellars. Gorgonzola is Italy's famous strong blue-veined cheese, which has been made in the little town of Gorgonzola near Milan since the early Middle Ages. It can be buttery and sweet (dolce) or firm, crumbly and quite salty (piccante). Mascarpone is a triple-cream pale, soft cheese made from crème fraîche. Sometimes buttermilk is added as well, depending on the brand. This is the basic ingredient used in many Italian desserts. Robiola di Roccaverano is a delicate, creamy cheese made in a very limited area in the north-western region of Piedmont. According to cheese connoisseurs, Robiola di Roccaverano made from pure goat's milk is one of the finest of all delicacies.

BELOW, LEFT TO RIGHT
Parmesan cheese, Fontina cheese and mortadella.

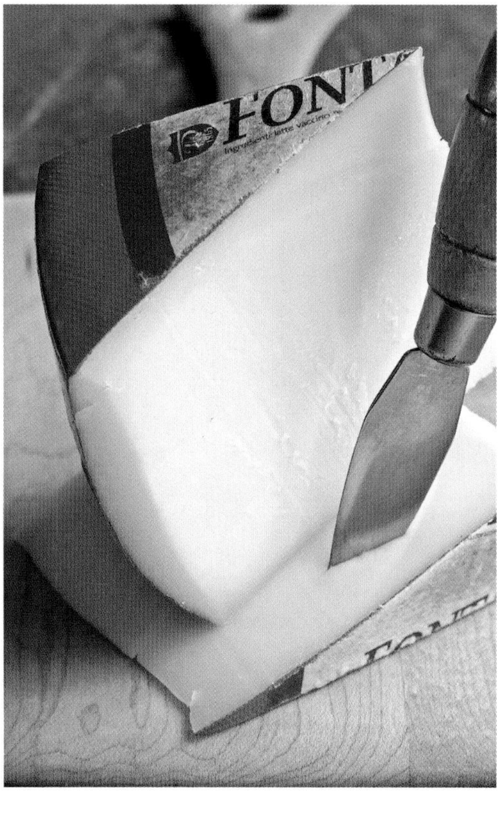

Butter is used extensively in the cooking of northern Italy, alongside olive oil, making much of the menu totally different to the predominantly olive oil-based meals of the southern regions. It is used in creamy risottos and drizzled over stuffed pasta dishes. It is also often the choice of fat for frying meat, giving a luxurious quality to the food.

Milk and cream are also used in many recipes, adding richness to pasta and gnocchi dishes, as well as being principal ingredients in the Piedmontese recipes Fonduta and Baked Egg and Cheese Custard.

MEAT AND GAME

Fresh meat, such as good quality beef, lamb, pork and especially veal, is taken for granted in northern Italy. The famous ragù Bolognese is made from a slow-cooked mixture of chopped pork, beef, prosciutto (ham), bacon and chicken livers, simmered for several hours in a rich and creamy tomato sauce. Chicken is popular in casseroles and fricassées. Veal cutlets make a very tasty dish which is typical of Milan, costolette alla Milanese. In this luxurious dish, they are flattened and cooked with a coating of rich buttery breadcrumbs.

Pride of place, however, goes to the traditional cured meats such as prosciutto crudo (ham), bresaola (beef) and mortadella (sausage). Prosciutto di Parma, or Parma ham, is simplicity itself: a joint of pork, salted and then cured by the fresh air descending from the Apennine mountains, refreshed by sea breezes, then aged in special aerated warehouses. It has a pure, unadulterated flavour, a silky consistency and a rich, salty taste.

FISH AND SHELLFISH

The Ligurian coast is the main focus of sea fish dishes in the north-west area of Italy. The Ligurian recipe for fish soup, ciuppin, uses all kinds of whole white fish in the simplest of stocks, with the addition of tomatoes, garlic and herbs, to make a delicate broth that is served with a couple of slices of white ciabatta bread at the bottom of the soup bowl.

Inland areas, however, make the most of freshwater fish, such as trout, tench and carp, which abound in the rivers and lakes of Lombardy. They are served in wonderful, flavoursome sauces that tend to be elegantly laced with white wine, garlic and herbs.

PASTA

Each region of Italy has its favourite pasta shapes, which are designed to work perfectly with the sauces of that region. Pansotti are triangle-shaped ravioli-style pasta pieces, stuffed with a mixture of vegetables, such as Swiss chard, borage and endive, and ricotta cheese; these are often served with pesto d'inverno, a delicious walnut pesto.

BELOW, LEFT TO RIGHT
Lamb cutlets, sea bass and tuna steaks.

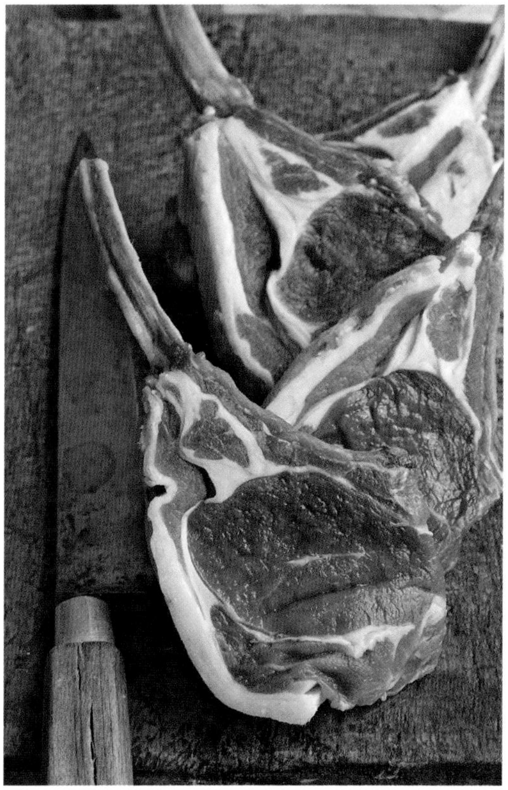

USING A PASTA MACHINE

1 Once you have made your pasta dough, it is important to allow it to rest under a clean cloth or wrapped in clear film (plastic wrap) for about 20 minutes. This will allow the gluten to relax and make the dough more manageable.

2 After the dough has rested, break off a piece about the size of a small fist. Always re-wrap the pasta you are not using. Use your hands to slightly flatten the piece you have broken off, then push it through the widest setting on your pasta machine.

3 Fold the dough in half and repeat. Do this until you hear the pasta 'snap' as the air is pressed out between the rollers; this indicates that the surface tension of the pasta is now correct.

4 Turn the machine to the next lower setting and put the sheet of pasta through the rollers twice.

5 Continue to push the pasta sheet twice through the rollers, at each of the settings, lowering it one setting at a time, until you get to the last or penultimate setting on the machine, depending on how fine you want the pasta to be.

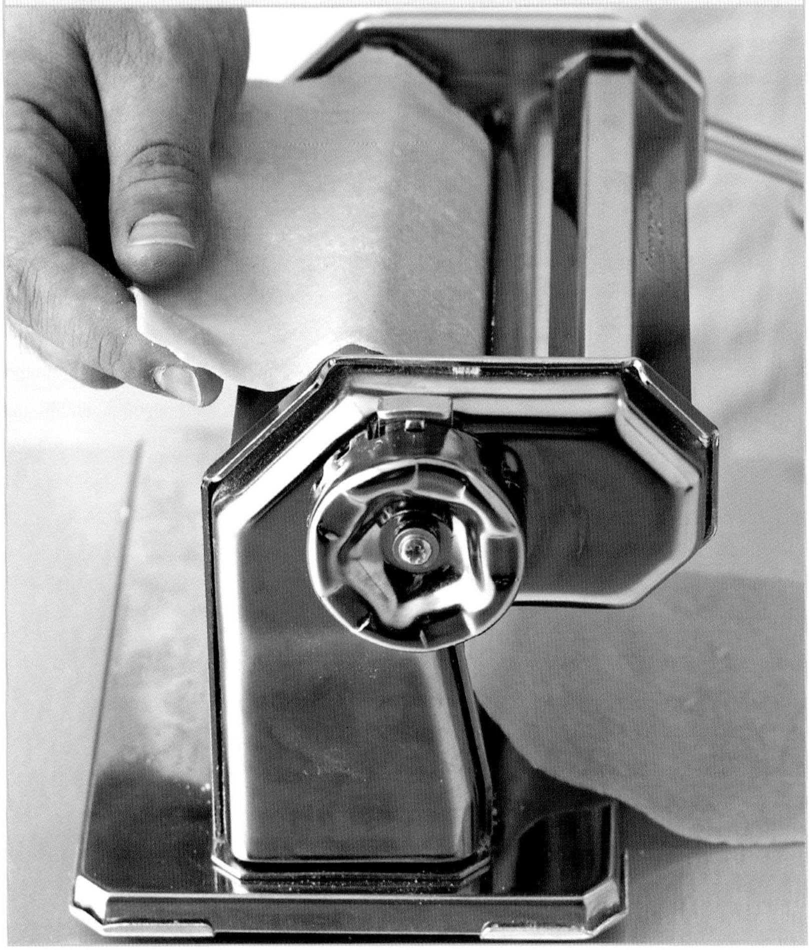

Trenette come in long, flat strips, either fresh or dried, and, like trofie, a spiral-shaped pasta, are sometimes served with boiled green beans, potatoes and pesto. Perhaps the most unusual pasta shapes of this region are croxetti, made in the shape of round medallions stamped with symbols. It is said that the women of Camogli in Liguria began making this pasta while their men were away at sea in order to pass the time.

RICE AND OTHER GRAINS

Italy is the leading producer of rice in Europe, with most rice being grown in the fertile Po valley. A steaming savoury risotto is a great base for serving whatever ingredients are in season, from seafood and wild mushrooms to meat and game. Lombardy and Piedmont produce short, barrel-shaped rice grains for risotto, and superfino rice is the favourite, although arborio is the most well known outside Italy.

In Roman times, polenta (pulmentum in Latin) was the staple food of the mighty Roman legions in this area of Italy. Over the next few centuries, buckwheat was introduced into Italy by the Saracens. This nutritious grain, known as grano saraceno, is still popular today for making polenta, mixed with maize meal, as it adds a distinctive flavour. Polenta is very hearty, and is a perfect base for tasty, protein-rich foods such as stews or melted cheese.

ABOVE, LEFT TO RIGHT
Trenette pasta, risotto rice, polenta and fennel.

RISOTTO ALLA MILANESE

The famous dish risotto alla Milanese gets its golden hue from the precious spice, saffron. Legend has it that the dish was invented when the painter of the stained-glass window of St Helen, in her yellow robes, in the Duomo of Milan presented a golden risotto infused with saffron as a gift to his boss's daughter for her wedding banquet.

Bread made from wheat flour is the normal accompaniment to every meal. But there are plenty of special breads that do more than soak up the olive oil and cooking juices. Flat breads such as focaccia are served in all kinds of flavours, or stuffed with delicious ingredients. Liguria's salty air and humidity makes it difficult to bake good bread that will stay fresh, so the Ligurians devised a focaccia that is best eaten hot out of the oven. This flat bread is usually topped with olive oil and salt, and in some areas, sage, rosemary, cheese or onions. Piadina, also known as piada or piè, first came into being as a simple peasant bread and is now the region's best-loved snack. This unleavened flat bread is best eaten piping hot, filled with greens, pan-fried vegetables, cheese and cured meats of all kinds, then folded in two, cut into four pieces or rolled up.

VEGETABLES AND FRUIT

As in most of Italy, certain fruits and vegetables are taken for granted – life would be unimaginable without them. Tomatoes are ubiquitous, appearing in almost every sauce, soup and casserole, not to mention pasta dishes. Both hot and sweet (bell) peppers are very popular in pasta sauces or thrown into a frittata. Courgettes (zucchini), fennel, artichokes and other sun-loving crops are grown in fields and gardens and eaten on a daily basis. Potatoes are eaten more than in the south of Italy as the damper, cooler climate suits their production. They are enjoyed in pasta dishes as well as on their own as a side dish.

The most luxurious ingredient found in this area is the white Alba truffle, which is the most delicious, expensive and sought-after truffle in the world, and its aromatic flavour enhances even the simplest dish. Finding and harvesting the truffles in the autumn, when they are at their peak, is a secretive, age-old process requiring a professional truffle hunter and his trained dog.

Fruits of all kinds abound in the benign climate of northern Italy. Peaches, apricots, cherries, apples, plums and pears all flourish in the clear, warm air of the mountain slopes of Piedmont and the Aosta Valley. The pear variety known as martin sec is grown here and makes a delicious dessert when cooked gently in red wine. Grapes flourish on the hills, and are made into world-famous wines.

HERBS, SEASONINGS AND SAUCES

Certain herbs and seasonings are characteristic of this part of Italy, usually because the climate suits their production. Basil can be tricky to grow, but the heat and fresh sea breezes of Liguria produce fantastic crops of this uniquely flavoured herb. Fresh Ligurian basil makes the best pesto in the world, if you ask the locals!

Aceto balsamico, or balsamic vinegar, is one of the key elements of the now world-famous Italian food culture. Just a few drops are all that is required to turn any dish into something special, from beef fillet to a chunk of Parmigiano Reggiano, and even strawberries and ice cream.

Mostarda di Cremona, from the inland port city of Cremona, consists of candied fruits, such as cherries, figs, slices of melon and pears, preserved in a mixture of sugar syrup and white mustard. The result is a tangy condiment that is served with meat, game or poultry dishes, or with cheese.

DRINKS

The sunny hillsides of the valley around Lake Iseo in Franciacorta, Lombardy, are covered with wonderful soil and have the perfect microclimate for growing the Pinot Bianco, Pinot Grigio, Pinot Nero and Chardonnay grapes used to make the local sparkling wines. Good-quality red, white and rosé wines are produced too, and altogether this region annually produces over 28 million gallons of wine.

At a first glance, the steep slopes of the Ligurian coast do not seem very hospitable to most agriculture, even vines, and yet about a hundred different varieties of grapes are cultivated in this small strip of mountainous land. The wines of Emilia-Romagna are generally less well known – the only truly famous wine of the region is Lambrusco, most of which is easy drinking, fizzy and sweet. The main grape grown in Piedmont is Nebbiolo, whose name derives from the word nebbia (fog). At the peak of ripening in September, heavy morning fog is a much hoped-for event, as the natural humidity improves the quality of the grapes, which are used to make a few renowned red wines, including the rather expensive and highly regarded Barolo.

AMARETTO DI SARONNO

This rich liqueur has a lineage dating back to the Renaissance. In 1525, the artist Bernardino Luini was commissioned to paint a fresco of the Madonna of the Miracles in Saronno. He chose as his model a beautiful local innkeeper, and in gratitude she prepared a special gift of apricot kernels steeped in brandy and presented the resulting concoction to the artist. This bittersweet amber-coloured liqueur is still popular today.

BELOW, LEFT TO RIGHT
Basil, mostarda di Cremona, Pinot Grigio and melted milk chocolate.

Many other alcoholic drinks are created in the northern regions. Vermouth was first made in the 17th century, and some claim that the classic Martini cocktail takes its name from the most well-known Italian producer of dry vermouth, Martini & Rossi. Punt e Mes is one of the world's most popular red vermouths, with a hint of wormwood and bitter herbs.

Fernet-Branca is a bitter, aromatic spirit made from a number of herbs and spices that can include myrrh, rhubarb, chamomile, cardamom, aloe and saffron.

Grappa, the clear spirit made by carefully distilling 'le raspe' (the skins, stalks and seeds) from grape pressings, is popular all over the north of Italy. A very strong, warming drink, it makes a good digestif for after a long, heavy meal.

CHOCOLATE

Piedmont, particularly the city of Turin, is the base for chocolate making in the northern regions. This chocolate is eaten just as it is, but it can also be used in all sorts of delicious desserts, such as chocolate pudding blended with coffee and amaretti, or in a dark rich cake, or combined with chestnut purée and meringues in a splendid confection known as Il Montebianco, or the white mountain.

PESTO

MAKES ABOUT 300ML/½PINT/1¼ CUPS

about 75g/3oz fresh basil leaves, washed but not bruised, dried carefully
large pinch of sea salt
3 cloves garlic, peeled and cut in half
100g/3¾oz pine kernels
25g/1oz/⅓ cup grated Parmesan or Pecorino (or a mixture of the two)
200ml/7fl oz/scant 1 cup extra virgin olive oil
sea salt and ground black pepper

1 Put the basil, salt and garlic into a mortar and crush with a pestle until reduced to a smooth green purée. Alternatively use a food processor.

2 Add the pine kernels and grated cheese and pound or process again until the pine kernels are all crushed.

3 Add the oil, a little at a time, stirring with a spoon, until you have reached a smooth, creamy texture. You may not need to use all of the oil.

4 Season with salt and pepper, and use as required.

COOK'S TIP The ingredients in this recipe do not need to be exact – taste the pesto as you prepare it so you can adjust or alter the quantities according to personal taste.

SOUPS AND ANTIPASTI

ZUPPE, MINESTRE E ANTIPASTI

The dish served as the first taste of a meal says a lot about the skill of the cook or host. It is essential to tune the palate to what is to follow. In the north of Italy, where a lot of food tends to be quite rich in butter and cheese, getting the appetizer right is vital, as it is likely to be followed by more than one rich course, including pasta or risotto. For this reason, it is important not to overload the stomach at the start of the meal. There is no shortage of cured meats in these regions, so many antipasti are meat based, even if it is only a plate of wafer-thin prosciutto di Parma (Parma ham), sliced immediately before serving, with nothing more than some crunchy grissini (breadsticks), the pride of Turin, or a few slices of truffle-infused salame to just whet the appetite.

PARMA HAM, PARMESAN AND OLIVE OIL FOCACCIA

The word that best describes the fashion-conscious city Milan is elegance, and the restaurants and food stores are as much a part of that as the fabulous shoe stores or the uber-chic haute-couture boutiques of the Via Montenapoleone. Milan is often where modern food trends begin and where cosmopolitan dishes sit happily alongside the ancient traditions of Milanese cuisine, and it is within the antipasto course where this is truly noticeable. The world-famous food emporium, Peck, in the heartland of the fashion centre sells food of the highest quality. This gastronomic institution has been here since 1883, and is respected all over the world. Peck is the benchmark by which the many other food stores all over this foodie city are judged.

The weather in north-western Italy ranges from one extreme to the other – freezing cold in the winter with miserable fog and snow, and blisteringly hot in the summer; both warming soups and light and fresh antipasti are on the menu. Hearty Minestrone Soup is a favourite in Lombardy and has now become popular throughout the world. Topped with a sprinkling of Parmesan cheese it makes a warming winter appetizer, but it can also be served cold on a hot summer's day.

Cured meats form an important part of the antipasto selection, including Cured Ham and Melon, which would always be made with prosciutto di Parma in Emilia-Romagna, and Bresaola with Parmesan and Rocket, which is drizzled with good-quality extra virgin olive oil.

Focaccia is closely linked to the cuisine of Liguria and Recco's Olive Oil Focaccia is one of the tastiest versions. The basic recipe can be changed with the addition of myriad other ingredients, too.

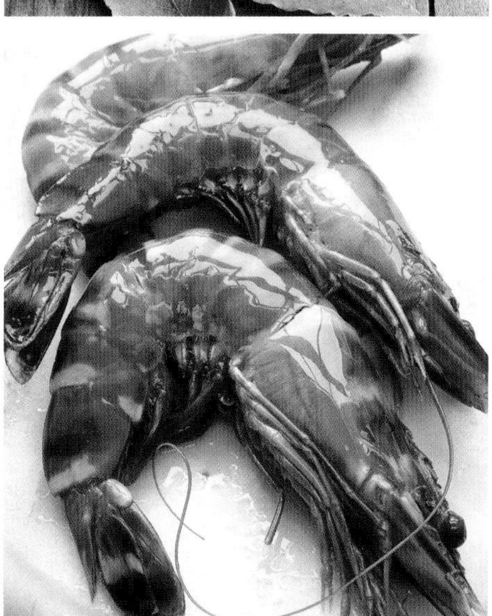

MINESTRONE SOUP
IL MINESTRONE

This comforting, substantial soup is one of the great specialities of Lombardy. Made with a combination of vegetables and beans, it can be thickened with rice, pasta or semolina to turn it into the 'big soup'. In summer it is served cold or at room temperature, and hot or cold it is delicious when finished off with a drizzle of extra virgin olive oil and a dusting of freshly grated Parmesan. If using dried borlotti beans, you will need to soak them overnight before you begin.

SERVES 6

200g/7oz fresh or dried borlotti beans, soaked overnight
about 1litre/1¾ pints/4 cups water or unsalted stock
60ml/4 tbsp olive oil
1 onion, finely chopped
45ml/3 tbsp chopped fresh flat leaf parsley
300g/11oz mixed green vegetables, such as spinach, cabbage, Swiss chard, lettuce leaves or spring greens (collards), chopped
2 courgettes (zucchini), chopped
1 potato, peeled and cubed
1 carrot, chopped
200g/7oz/1¾ cups short stubby pasta, or 200g/7oz/1 cup long grain rice
salt and ground black pepper
30–45ml/2–3 tbsp freshly grated Parmesan cheese, to serve

1 If using dried beans, put the soaked beans in a pan and cover with cold water. Bring to the boil and boil fast for 5 minutes. Drain and rinse.

2 Put the fresh or boiled, dried beans in a pan and cover generously with water or unsalted stock. Bring to the boil, then simmer for up to 30 minutes, adding more water or stock if too much of the liquid evaporates, until tender: the cooked beans should not be falling apart, and there should be about 550ml/18fl oz/2½ cups liquid left at the end of the cooking time.

3 Heat the oil in a large pan and fry the onion gently for 5 minutes, or until soft. Strain the cooked beans, reserving the liquid. Add the beans to the onion and stir together well.

4 Add the parsley, the green vegetables, courgettes, potato and carrot.

5 Fry together gently, adding 45ml/3 tbsp liquor from the boiled beans to moisten. Cook for 40 minutes, until the vegetables are starting to soften, then pour in the remaining bean liquor to cover, reduce the heat and simmer slowly for 30 minutes, stirring often, until the vegetables are soft. Add more liquid if necessary.

6 Season to taste and add the pasta or rice. Cook gently until the pasta or rice is cooked.

7 Remove from the heat, and allow to stand for 5–10 minutes. Ladle into soup bowls and serve sprinkled with a little Parmesan cheese.

COOK'S TIP

Do not add salt to the water until the beans are tender, as it will cause the skins to shrivel and harden.

PER PORTION Energy 386kcal/1625kJ; Protein 15g; Carbohydrate 54g, of which sugars 5g; Fat 13g, of which saturates 3g; Cholesterol 5mg; Calcium 171mg; Fibre 3.2g; Sodium 111mg.

SERVES 4

$^1/_2$ tomato
4 large red or yellow (bell) peppers
250ml/8fl oz/1 cup milk
10 garlic cloves, peeled and left whole
150ml/$^1/_4$ pint/$^2/_3$ cup olive oil
10 anchovies preserved in salt, cleaned and boned
50g/2oz/$^1/_4$ cup unsalted butter
45ml/3 tbsp double (heavy) cream
ground black pepper

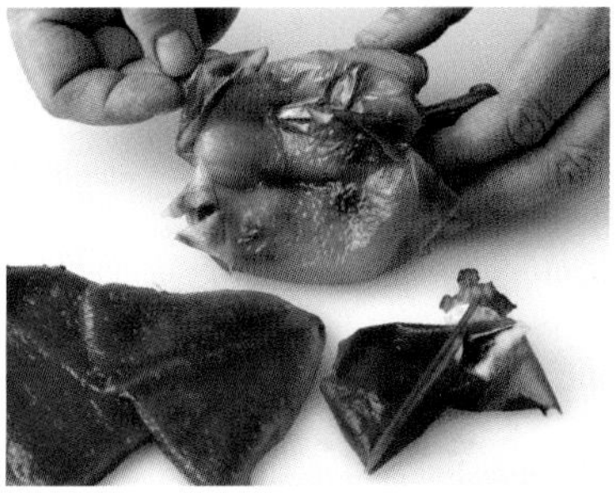

BAGNA CAODA WITH ROASTED PEPPERS
BAGNA CAODA CON PEPERONI

The delicious Piedmontese speciality, bagna caoda, is traditionally served as a hot sauce in a glazed terracotta container warmed over a night-light, into which vegetables are dipped. In this more elegant version, the potently flavoured sauce (which literally translates as 'hot bath') is used to smother roasted sweet peppers. The classic dip is served to celebrate the end of the grape harvest, and the final dregs are added to beaten eggs, which would then be scrambled and scooped up with hunks of bread.

1 Plunge the tomato into boiling water for 30 seconds, then refresh in cold water. Peel away the skin, then chop the flesh.

2 Put the peppers under a hot grill (broiler), turning occasionally, until blackened and burnt all over. Put them on a board and cover with an upturned bowl. Leave to cool.

3 Peel and remove the seeds from the peppers and cut the flesh into neat strips. Arrange the pepper strips on a platter and keep them to one side while you make the bagna caoda.

4 In a small pan, cook the milk with the garlic over a low heat until the garlic is completely softened, then mash the garlic into the milk.

5 Put the oil in a pan and add the anchovies. Heat slowly over a low heat, stirring, until the anchovies have dissolved into the oil, then stir in the butter and add pepper to taste.

6 Whisk the milk and garlic into the anchovy mixture, then add the chopped tomato and cream. Stir and heat through briefly until hot. Serve the sauce, poured over the sliced roasted peppers.

COOK'S TIP

The sauce should be served as a dip, with raw and cooked vegetables, cut into pieces for easy dipping.

PER PORTION Energy 559kcal/2312kJ; Protein 3g; Carbohydrate 15g, of which sugars 13g; Fat 55g, of which saturates 16g; Cholesterol 44mg; Calcium 26mg; Fibre 3.6g; Sodium 13mg.

BAKED CHICKPEA FLOUR PANCAKES
LA FARINATA

When you first make farinata you will be more than a little alarmed at quite how liquid the batter seems to be. Fear not, it will pull together quite magically into a smooth pancake as it bakes. This is the cheapest of foods – just finely ground chickpeas, water, oil, salt and pepper – and yet it manages to be utterly moreish. Farinata is wonderful with Stracchino cheese, or with salame, or just by itself – but it's always best served warm from the oven.

SERVES 6

225g/8oz/2 cups chickpea flour
60ml/4 tbsp olive oil
1.5 litres/2½ pints/6¼ cups water
sea salt and ground black pepper

1 Put the chickpea flour into a large mixing bowl and add the water. Mix together thoroughly using a whisk. Season with salt and ground black pepper, then add half the olive oil.

2 Leave the farinata mixture to stand for at least 1 hour or preferably overnight.

3 Preheat the oven to 200°C/400°F/Gas 6. Use the remaining oil to grease a shallow baking tray and pour in the farinata mixture to a depth of no more than 2.5cm/1in.

4 Bake for 30 minutes, or until crisp on the outside but still soft in the middle. Slice into wide strips and roll up, then serve while warm.

PER PORTION Energy 202kcal/868kJ; Protein 7g; Carbohydrate 19g, of which sugars 1g; Fat 12g, of which saturates 2g; Cholesterol 0mg; Calcium 68mg; Fibre 4g; Sodium 15mg.

CURED HAM AND MELON
PROSCIUTTO E MELONE

This is the ultimate Italian antipasto and it remains a sure-fire winner every time it is served, as long as the melon is perfectly ripe and sweet, the figs are soft and a little sticky, and the ham is freshly and expertly sliced into paper-thin sheets. This fresh combination was originally discovered in Emilia-Romagna, where this dish originates. Off-season, when the melons and figs are not available, the fruit of choice would be ripe pears. Serve it with fresh, crusty bread and chilled rosé on a sunny day.

SERVES 4

75g/3oz salad leaves
1 melon, about 1.2kg/2½lb, chilled
4 figs, either green or black, chilled
12 slices prosciutto crudo (prosciutto di Parma, prosciutto di San Daniele or prosciutto di Carpegna) or speck

1 Arrange the salad leaves on a large serving platter. Slice and seed the melon and arrange it on the salad leaves.

2 If the figs are firm, peel off their skins, otherwise leave the skin on.

3 Quarter the figs and arrange them alongside the melon slices.

4 Arrange the prosciutto slices in the centre of the dish, overlapping the melon slices and figs, then serve immediately.

PER PORTION Energy 392kcal/1661kJ; Protein 57g; Carbohydrate 19g, of which sugars 19g; Fat 10g, of which saturates 3g; Cholesterol 174mg; Calcium 74mg; Fibre 2.2g; Sodium 3647mg.

BRESAOLA WITH PARMESAN AND ROCKET
BRESAOLA CON PARMIGIANO E RUCOLA

Intensely and uniformly red in colour with a delicate, slightly salty aroma, bresaola is the only Italian cured meat made from specially selected beef haunches. The beef is seasoned with a special mixture of salt, pepper and other spices, then cured under controlled humidity and temperature. The finished product is put inside pork gut casings and cured for a further period of between one and three months. The tradition of bresaola spans several centuries and is a product of the area of Lombardy called Valtellina. Once sliced, bresaola has a bright red colouring and a well-defined flavour. Traditionally, it is served sliced paper thin, with a dressing of olive oil, lemon juice and pepper, and accompanied by some good bread.

1 Arrange the bresaola on a serving platter in a single layer, slightly overlapping the slices.

2 Drizzle with a little olive oil; not too much, however, just enough to give the meat a shiny appearance.

3 Drizzle with the lemon juice or balsamic vinegar, and sprinkle with black pepper.

4 Cover with the rocket leaves, and sprinkle over the Parmesan cheese shavings. Add a final drizzle of olive oil and serve immediately.

SERVES 4

200g/7oz bresaola, thinly sliced
extra virgin olive oil, to drizzle
juice of ½ lemon or 10ml/2 tsp best-quality balsamic vinegar
75g/3oz rocket (arugula) leaves
75g/3oz/1 cup Parmesan cheese, shaved
ground black pepper

PER PORTION Energy 307kcal/1275kJ; Protein 35g; Carbohydrate 1g, of which sugars 1g; Fat 18g, of which saturates 5g; Cholesterol 17mg; Calcium 222mg; Fibre 0.2g; Sodium 142mg.

SERVES 6

1 rabbit, jointed, approx 1.8kg/4lb
15ml/1 tbsp vinegar
2 carrots
2 celery sticks
1 onion
1 sprig rosemary
2 garlic cloves, thinly sliced
8 bay leaves
8 juniper berries
12 black peppercorns
sea salt
about 600ml/1 pint/2½ cups extra virgin olive oil

PER PORTION Energy 468kcal/1937kJ; Protein 28g; Carbohydrate 4g, of which sugars 3g; Fat 38g, of which saturates 7g; Cholesterol 106mg; Calcium 67mg; Fibre 1.1g; Sodium 76mg.

RABBIT ANTIPASTO
ANTIPASTO DI CONIGLIO

A lovely recipe from Piedmont, this antipasto needs to be prepared about 3 days in advance. It ends up like a rustic version of a terrine and is absolutely delicious served with hunks of crusty bread to mop up the juices. Rabbit meat is cheap and tasty, and very low in fat. The flavour and tenderness are greatly improved by soaking overnight, or at least for a few hours, in water and vinegar. Wild rabbit is best soaked in milk due to the intensity of its aroma and taste.

1 Put the jointed rabbit into a large bowl and cover with water. Add the vinegar and leave overnight.

2 The next day, put the carrots, celery, onion and rosemary into a large pan, and cover with water and bring to the boil.

3 Add the jointed rabbit and return to the boil. Reduce the heat and simmer gently for 90 minutes, or until the rabbit is cooked through and completely tender. Turn off the heat and leave the rabbit to cool down completely in the stock.

4 When the rabbit is cold, remove all the meat from the bones.

5 Put a quarter of the meat in a layer in the base of a terrine and cover with a quarter of the sliced garlic, bay leaves, juniper berries and black peppercorns, and a sprinkling of salt.

6 Repeat the layering process with the remaining ingredients, creating four layers. Cover with olive oil, and chill for 2–3 days.

7 Serve on a platter, removing the garlic slices, peppercorns and bay leaves as you eat.

SERVES 4

300g/11oz/4$^{1}/_{2}$ cups mixed mushrooms, such as button (white), brown cap (cremini), chestnut, porcini and oyster, thinly sliced
200g/7oz mortadella, sliced and cut into sticks
115g/4oz/1$^{1}/_{4}$ cups Parmesan cheese, shaved
juice of $^{1}/_{2}$ lemon
15ml/1 tbsp chopped fresh mint
60ml/4 tbsp chopped flat leaf parsley
60ml/4 tbsp extra virgin olive oil
sea salt and ground black pepper

MORTADELLA, MUSHROOMS AND PARMESAN
MORTADELLA, FUNGHETTI E PARMIGIANO

A large Italian sausage made of finely ground heat-cured pork, mortadella incorporates at least 15 per cent small cubes of pork fat (principally the hard fat from the neck). It is delicately flavoured with spices, including black pepper, myrtle berries, nutmeg, coriander and pistachio nuts and/or olives. Although other versions are made throughout Italy, mortadella originated in Bologna, the capital of Emilia-Romagna, and this is why the American version is given the name bologna or baloney sausage.

1 Put the mushrooms, the mortadella and the Parmesan cheese in a shallow bowl and mix together.

2 In a separate bowl mix together the lemon juice, mint and parsley, and then season with salt and pepper.

3 Add the oil to the dressing mixture and whisk thoroughly until it thickens. Adjust the seasoning to taste.

4 Pour the dressing over the salad ingredients. Toss together gently, then divide among plates and serve immediately.

COOK'S TIP

For an elegant occasion, you can arrange the mushrooms in one layer on a pretty plate, then cover with a layer of mortadella, sprinkle on the dressing and finish off with the Parmesan cheese shavings.

PER PORTION Energy 429kcal/1776kJ; Protein 19g; Carbohydrate 1g, of which sugars 1g; Fat 39g, of which saturates 14g; Cholesterol 64mg; Calcium 325mg; Fibre 0.6g; Sodium 655mg.

LIGURIAN SEAFOOD SALAD

INSALATA DI FRUTTI DI MARE ALLA LIGURE

The shellfish and crustaceans used for this delicious salad can vary according to availability, as long as whatever you use is perfectly fresh and sweet to the taste. Razor shells, queen scallops, crab or small chunks of monkfish tail all work well.

SERVES 4

200g/7oz squid, cleaned (see Cook's Tip) and cut into strips and rings
1kg/2¼lb mussels
1kg/2¼lb baby clams
175g/6oz/1½ cups small raw prawns (shrimp)
4 large raw prawns (shrimp)
45ml/3 tbsp chopped flat leaf parsley, plus extra to garnish
juice of ½ lemon
90ml/6 tbsp extra virgin olive oil
sea salt and ground black pepper
lemon wedges, to serve

1 Boil the squid in salted water for 25–30 minutes, or until tender.

2 Meanwhile, scrub the mussels and clams with a stiff brush and rise well. Discard any mussels that remain open after being sharply tapped. Scrape off any barnacles and remove the 'beards' with a small knife. Rinse well.

3 Put the mussels and clams into a large pan. Cover and steam for 8 minutes. The shells will open; discard any that remain closed.

4 Put the small prawns in a pan and cover with cold water. Bring to the boil and cook for 1 minute. Drain them and allow to cool, then remove their shells.

5 Remove the mussels from their shells and put them in a large bowl with the small prawns and squid. Mix together and set aside.

6 Cook the large prawns in a pan of boiling water for 2 minutes, then drain. Make a shallow cut down the centre of the curved back of each prawn. Pull out the black vein with a cocktail stick (toothpick) or your fingers, then rinse each prawn thoroughly. Leave to cool.

7 Add the parsley to the seafood, squeeze over the lemon juice, then add the oil and some pepper. Mix well and adjust the seasoning to taste. Distribute between four plates, adding one large prawn to each. Serve sprinkled with extra parsley and lemon wedges.

COOK'S TIP

To prepare squid yourself, wash it carefully, rinsing off any ink that remains on the body. Holding the body firmly, pull away the head and tentacles. If the ink sac is still intact, remove it and discard. Pull out all the innards including the long transparent 'pen'. Peel off and discard the thin purple skin on the body, as well as the two small side fins. Slice across the head just under the eyes, reserving the tentacles. Discard the rest of the head. Squeeze the tentacles at the head end to push out the round beak in the centre and discard. Rinse the pouch and tentacles well.

PER PORTION Energy 697kcal/2921kJ; Protein 96g; Carbohydrate 12g, of which sugars 0g; Fat 30g, of which saturates 5g; Cholesterol 578mg; Calcium 370mg; Fibre 0.1g; Sodium 3971mg.

RECCO'S OLIVE OIL FOCACCIA
FOCACCIA DI RECCO ALL'OLIO

Focaccia is widely associated with Ligurian cuisine and this focaccia from Recco is legendary. The story goes that during the 16th and 17th centuries, when Recco was an easy target for bandit attacks, men defended their lands, while women left for the hinterland with the children and elders, taking with them wheat, oil and salt. Once they felt safe, they kneaded the wheat with the stream water and bartered salt and oil for some cheese. Elders, who used to gather the wood and light up the fires, started leaning some slate over the burning coals to cook the mixture, and the focaccia was born. There are many versions of this famous bread in Recco and the fourth Sunday in May is the annual Recco Focaccia Festival.

SERVES 4

350ml/12fl oz/1½ cups warm water
40g/1½oz fresh yeast
500g/1¼lb/5 cups unbleached strong white bread flour
30ml/2 tbsp extra virgin olive oil, plus extra for drizzling
10g/¼oz salt
25g/1oz coarse salt

1 Pour half the water into a small bowl and stir in the yeast. Leave in a warm place for 15 minutes, or until frothy.

2 Put the flour into a large bowl and add the olive oil and the 10g/¼oz salt. Pour in the yeast mixture and remaining water, and stir together well.

3 Knead the dough for 20 minutes, or until soft and stretchy. The dough should be quite wet, but it shouldn't feel sticky. Put the dough in a large, well-oiled bowl, cover loosely with clear film (plastic wrap) and leave to rise in a warm place for about 1 hour.

4 Knock back (punch down) the dough. Brush the base of a 40 x 60cm/16 x 24in tin (pan) generously with olive oil and then flatten the dough out over the base to cover it completely. Using your fingers, splash the surface with some water (or spray using an atomizer), then sprinkle over some coarse salt and drizzle with lots of olive oil (be generous with the oil).

5 Using your fingertips, make lots of deep dimples all over the surface of the dough. Leave the dough to rise in a warm, draught-free place for 2 hours, or until doubled in volume. After 1½ hours preheat the oven to 200°C/400°F/Gas 6.

6 Bake the focaccia for 10 minutes in the preheated oven, during which time it will absorb all the olive oil on the surface. Drizzle over a little more olive oil, then bake for a further 20–25 minutes, or until the focaccia is golden in colour.

7 Immediately remove the focaccia from the tin and allow it to cool slightly on a wire rack. Serve while still slightly warm.

VARIATIONS

- For an onion focaccia, finely chop ½ red onion and add the onion to the mixture at step 2. Very finely slice ½ red onion and sprinkle over the top of the focaccia during the last 10–15 minutes of cooking time.
- For a rosemary focaccia, sprinkle a few sprigs of fresh rosemary over the top of the focaccia when you add the coarse salt and oil.
- For the classic focaccia al formaggio, divide the dough in half and spread the first half over the base of the tin. Cover with Stracchino or Crescenza cheese – a sour, stretched-curd cheese – and then cover with the second sheet of dough, rolled out to fit over the first. Finish off as above.

PER PORTION Energy 511kcal/2163kJ; Protein 18g; Carbohydrate 94g, of which sugars 2g; Fat 9g, of which saturates 1g; Cholesterol 0mg; Calcium 184mg; Fibre 3.9g; Sodium 3448mg.

TOMATO AND ANCHOVY PIZZA
PIZZA DELL'ANDREA

This type of pizza, which is similar to pissaladière from the South of France, is very popular throughout Liguria, but especially in Imperia, Diano Marino and Bordighera. It is also enjoyed in Sanremo, but here has been re-christened 'sardenea', or 'pizza with sardines'. The name is reputed to come from the name of Andrea Doria, 1466–1560, a celebrated local hero and ruler of Oneglia, who reputedly was very fond of this dish. You can make it with fresh sardines instead of anchovies.

SERVES 6

600g/1lb 5oz/5¼ cups strong white bread flour
about 300ml/½ pint/1¼ cups luke warm water
40g/1½oz fresh yeast
60ml/4 tbsp olive oil
large pinch of sea salt

FOR THE TOPPING

2 small onions, finely sliced
200ml/7fl oz/scant 1 cup olive oil, plus extra for drizzling
1kg/2¼lb fresh ripe tomatoes, seeded
115g/4oz salted anchovies, rinsed and boned
leaves from 2 fresh basil sprigs
12 pitted black olives, or 30ml/2 tbsp salted capers, rinsed and dried
2 garlic cloves, thinly sliced

1 Pile the flour on to the work surface, make a hole in the centre using your fist and pour in enough lukewarm water to just fill the hollow. Crumble the yeast into the hollow and mix together gently then leave for a few minutes and mix again. Continue this gentle mixing and resting for 10 minutes, or until the dough is just fizzing and soft.

2 Add the olive oil and salt, and knead together, adding more lukewarm water as required to create a soft, elastic ball of dough. Kneading will take at least 15 minutes in total.

3 Shape the dough into a ball and place it in a lightly oiled bowl. Cover loosely with clear film (plastic wrap), or with a clean floured cloth. Leave to rise in a warm, draught-free place for 2–3 hours.

4 Meanwhile, make the topping. Fry the onions gently in a little olive oil until pale golden in colour. Add the tomatoes and simmer for 30 minutes, or until the sauce is glossy and thickened.

5 Add the anchovies to the tomato sauce. Continue to simmer for a further 5–10 minutes. Then remove from the heat.

6 Preheat the oven to 240°C/475°F/Gas 9. Generously oil one large or two small shallow baking trays.

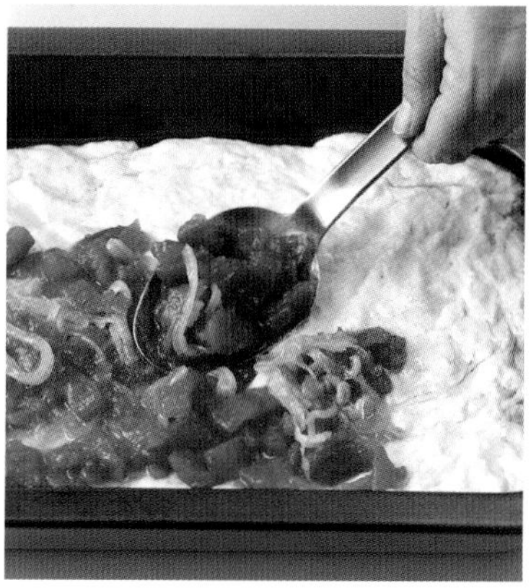

7 Using your fingers, spread out the risen dough over the tray(s) so that it is 1cm/½in thick.

8 Spread the tomato sauce over the surface of the dough, then add the basil leaves, olives or capers and the sliced garlic. Drizzle a little oil over the top.

9 Bake for 30 minutes, or until the pizza is crisp and golden around the edges. Serve hot or cold, sliced into rectangular pieces.

PER PORTION Energy 813kcal/3402kJ; Protein 19g; Carbohydrate 82g, of which sugars 8g; Fat 48g, of which saturates 7g; Cholesterol 12mg; Calcium 22mg; Fibre 5.3g; Sodium 908mg.

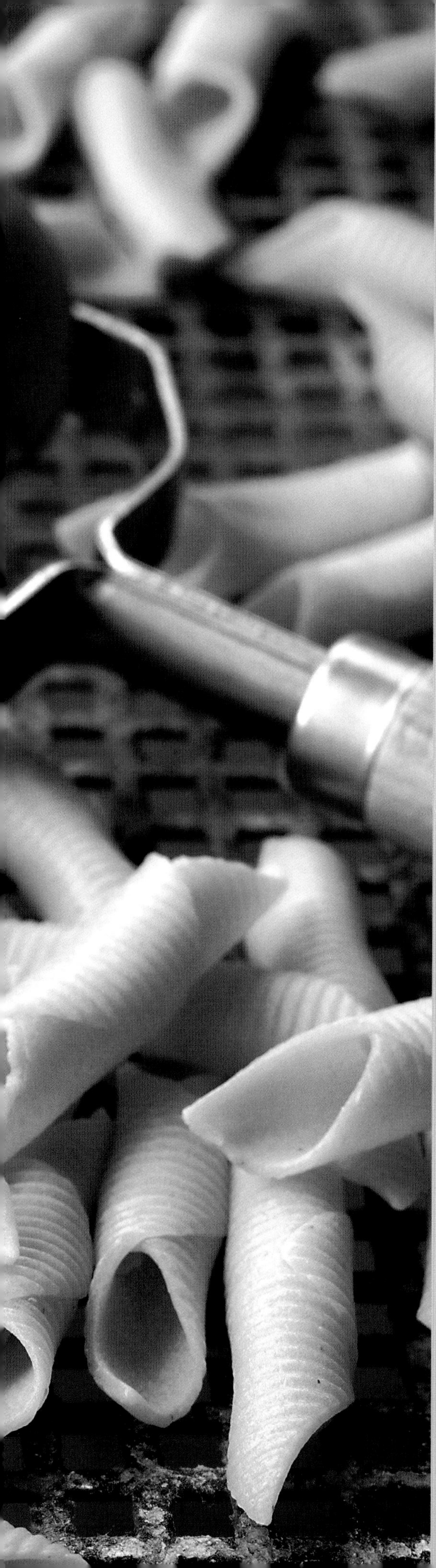

PASTA, GNOCCHI RICE AND POLENTA

PASTA, GNOCCHI, RISO E POLENTA

Emilia-Romagna is the birthplace of fresh pasta (known here as la sfoglia) so tagliatelle, tortellini, lasagna and cannelloni appear on every menu with a multitude of delicious sauces. The Classic Ragù Bolognese is famous the world over. Farther north, in Lombardy and Piedmont, it is really risotto that takes over as the primo of choice, from the simplest ones with nothing more than good chicken stock, plenty of fresh butter and grated Parmesan cheese, to more substantial options containing sausages, beans, vegetables and cheeses, as well as extravagant ingredients such as truffles and saffron. Gnocchi and polenta are offered on the menus of these regions, particularly during cold winter months. Here, as elsewhere in Italy, the primo is the most important course of the meal, following a light antipasto and preceding a meat or fish course.

FRESH EGG PASTA AND LUXURIOUS RISOTTOS

Traditionally, an Italian meal in the north would consist of a light antipasto, followed by a substantial primo of pasta, risotto, polenta or gnocchi, and then a meat or fish course would follow as a secondo. These days, unless it is a celebration meal of some kind, the size of those traditional meals is often reduced, and many people opt for just a plate of pasta or risotto with perhaps a salad to follow rather than all the courses.

Whereas the south favours dried durum wheat pasta, the north (in particular Emilia-Romagna) favours fresh egg pasta, especially for special occasions, although there is still a wide consumption of dried pasta tossed with a sauce, known as a pastasciutta. Many local cheeses and cured meats are combined with pasta, polenta or risotto, which makes these dishes especially filling.

It may be reassuring for all those cooks who have found cooking risotto to be a bit tricky, to know that risotto comes in a whole range of different textures in these regions, with the dish being slightly less liquid in the north-west, definitely food to be enjoyed with a fork. By contrast, in Venice, the most traditional local risotto dishes can be almost soup-like in texture and often eaten with a spoon. There is no rule regarding texture – it can vary enormously depending upon where it is made and which other component ingredients have gone into making it. There is also much attention paid to the variety of risotto rice used. Carnaroli, with its big, fat dense grains, is considered to be a very special variety that needs to be combined with extravagent ingredients such as truffle, lobster or Prosecco, whereas the humble Arborio is used in everyday cooking.

CHEESE AND MUSHROOM CANNELLONI
CANNELLONI AI FUNGHI E FORMAGGIO

This is a very rich version of this classic baked pasta dish, made lighter with the addition of a tomato sauce and some fresh basil. Vary the taste of this perfect supper recipe by using different kinds of mushrooms and cheese.

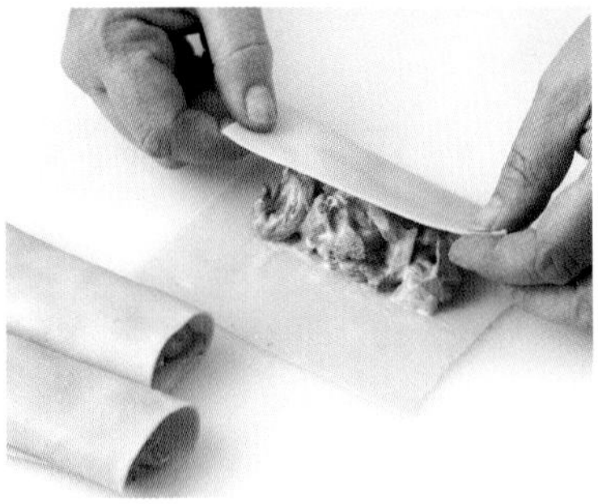

1 Preheat the oven to 160°C/325°F/Gas 3. Brush the butter over the base and sides of a large shallow ovenproof dish.

2 Blanch the pasta sheets in salted boiling water and drop them into cold water to prevent them sticking to each other.

3 Heat the oil in a pan and add the garlic. Fry until the garlic is just pungent, then discard. Add the chopped onions and the mushrooms to the garlicky oil. Cook for 5–10 minutes or until softened.

4 Transfer the onions and mushrooms to a mixing bowl, season with salt and pepper, and gently stir in the cream cheese.

5 Take a sheet of pasta, drain and blot carefully. Place it flat on a board and add a tablespoonful of the mushroom filling. Roll the pasta up and place in the buttered dish. Repeat with the remaining pasta sheets and filling.

6 To make the sauce, melt the butter in a separate pan and add the tomatoes. Simmer for about 10 minutes. Season and add the cream, half the Parmesan cheese and the basil, then remove from the heat.

7 Pour the sauce over the filled cannelloni. Sprinkle with the remaining Parmesan cheese and bake for 15–20 minutes, until golden and bubbling. Leave to stand for 5 minutes before serving with extra Parmesan and basil on top.

SERVES 4

25g/1oz/2 tbsp butter, melted
250g/9oz fresh pasta sheets
45ml/3 tbsp olive oil
1 garlic clove, lightly crushed
3 small onions, chopped
500g/1¼lb/8 cups mushrooms, roughly chopped
115g/4oz/½ cup cream cheese

FOR THE SAUCE

25g/1oz/2 tbsp unsalted butter
250g/9oz drained canned tomatoes, seeded and coarsely chopped
200ml/7fl oz/scant 1 cup single (light) cream
150g/5oz/1½ cups grated Parmesan cheese, plus extra to serve
8 fresh basil leaves, torn, plus extra to serve
sea salt and ground black pepper

PER PORTION Energy 787kcal/3279kJ; Protein 27g; Carbohydrate 42g, of which sugars 7g; Fat 58g, of which saturates 30g; Cholesterol 117mg; Calcium 526mg; Fibre 2.5g; Sodium 472mg.

SERVES 4

250g/9oz potatoes, peeled and cut into 2.5cm/1in cubes
250g/9oz green beans, trimmed and cut into 2.5cm/1in lengths
300g/11oz trenette
1 x quantity Pesto (see page 21)
40g/1½oz pine nuts, lightly toasted
sea salt
grated Parmesan cheese, to serve

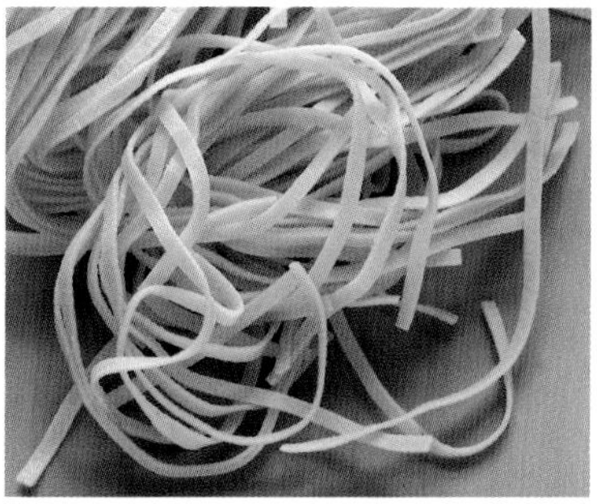

TRENETTE WITH PESTO IN THE GENOESE STYLE
TRENETTE AL PESTO ALLA GENOVESE

For Ligurians, there are only two pasta shapes that, along with potato gnocchi, are acceptable for use when it comes to serving their green basil pesto, and these are: trenette (long thin ribbons, often made with a little chopped borage blended into the dough) and trofie (the local, short corkscrew-shape). Pesto is traditionally made towards the end of the summer in large amounts, when the basil plants are flowering and at their most pungent, and it is then preserved for the winter months. Many different versions of the basic sauce exist; the recipes vary from household to household. This traditional way of enjoying the pasta together with pesto, potatoes and beans is typical of the city of Genoa.

1 Boil the potatoes and steam the green beans until tender.

2 Bring a large pan of salted water to the boil, add the trenette and cook according to the packet instructions. When there are 3 minutes of cooking time remaining, add the cooked potatoes and beans to heat them through.

3 Reserve 45ml/3 tbsp of the cooking liquid, then drain the pasta and vegetables. Add the reserved liquid to the pesto and stir to dilute.

4 Add the pasta and vegetables to the pesto and toss together well. Serve immediately, with the toasted pine nuts sprinkled over and a sprinkling of Parmesan cheese.

PER PORTION Energy 1049kcal/4364kJ; Protein 19g; Carbohydrate 72g, of which sugars 5g; Fat 78g, of which saturates 10g; Cholesterol 6mg; Calcium 160mg; Fibre 5.3g; Sodium 62mg.

SERVES 4

12 sheets fresh lasagne
3 medium potatoes, peeled
50g/2oz/1/4 cup unsalted butter
50g/2oz/1/2 cup plain (all-purpose) flour
600ml/1 pint/2 1/2 cups milk
60ml/4 tbsp Pesto (see page 21)
115g/4oz/1 1/4 cups grated Parmesan cheese
sea salt and ground black pepper
small leaf basil or torn basil leaves, to garnish

LASAGNA WITH PESTO AND POTATOES
LASAGNA AL PESTO CON LE PATATE

The combination of potatoes and pesto is a classic one, and the addition of the pasta, cheese and creamy sauce here turns it all into a lovely dense, rich dish which makes a perfect vegetarian lunch or supper dish. Serve with a salad, if you like.

1 Blanch the pasta sheets in salted boiling water and drop them into cold water to prevent them sticking to each other. Lay them out ready to use. Do not let them overlap, or they will stick together.

2 Boil the potatoes until soft. Drain and then slice them thinly. Preheat the oven to 190°C/375°F/Gas 5.

3 Melt the butter in a pan until foaming, add the flour and stir together vigorously until a smooth roux is formed. Add the milk and stir together thoroughly. Simmer gently, stirring frequently until the sauce is thickened enough to coat the back of a spoon.

4 Stir in half the pesto and season with salt and pepper. Add about half the Parmesan cheese and stir again.

5 Spread a layer of the sauce over the base of a shallow ovenproof dish. Cover with a layer of potatoes, then add a layer of sauce, and dot with some of the remaining pesto. Cover with lasagne sheets and another layer of sauce, then a few dots of pesto. Sprinkle with Parmesan.

6 Repeat the layering process, finishing off with a layer of sauce. Sprinkle the remaining Parmesan on top and bake for 20–30 minutes, until bubbling and golden. Serve sprinkled with basil and extra Parmesan.

PER PORTION Energy 600kcal/2526kJ; Protein 26g; Carbohydrate 61g, of which sugars 9g; Fat 30g, of which saturates 16g; Cholesterol 71mg; Calcium 591mg; Fibre 2.9g; Sodium 367mg.

RICOTTA RAVIOLI

RAVIOLI CON RIPIENO DI RICOTTA

This is one of the simplest and most delicious of all the filled pasta recipes from Emilia-Romagna. Like a lot of classic Italian dishes, it relies on the absolute freshness and quality of ingredients, in this case, ricotta.

SERVES 6

400g/14oz/1¾ cups ricotta cheese
pinch of grated nutmeg
175g/6oz/2 cups grated Parmesan cheese
6 eggs
250g/9oz/2¼ cups plain (all-purpose) flour
200g/7oz/generous 1 cup fine semolina
1.5ml/¼ tsp olive oil
150g/5oz/10 tbsp unsalted butter
5 fresh sage leaves, rubbed gently between your palms to release their flavour
sea salt and ground black pepper

1 Put the ricotta cheese in a bowl and mix in the nutmeg, half the Parmesan cheese and season with salt and pepper. Add an egg and blend the mixture together. Set aside.

2 Put the flour and semolina on to the worktop and make a hollow in the centre using your fist. Break the remaining 5 eggs into the hole. Stir the eggs into the dry ingredients, then begin to knead together. Add the olive oil and knead until you have a smooth, elastic dough. Rest the dough under a clean cloth or wrap in clear film (plastic wrap) for 20 minutes.

3 Roll out the dough thinly until fine, silky and cool. Divide it lengthways into 6cm/2½in wide strips. Work on one strip at a time, covering the other with a slightly damp cloth.

4 Drop 5ml/1 tsp of the ricotta cheese mixture in heaps along one half of each strip, leaving a gap of two fingers between each one.

5 Fold the strip in half, over the filling, encasing the filling at one side. Using a pastry (cookie) cutter or an upturned glass, cut around each section of filled pasta to make a crescent with a straight edge. Seal the curved edge of each crescent with the prongs of a fork. Continue in this way until all the dough has been cut.

6 Bring a large pan of salted water to a rolling boil. Drop the ravioli into the water and boil until floating on the surface and tender. Remove the ravioli with a slotted spoon, and arrange in a warmed serving dish.

7 Meanwhile, melt the butter with the sage leaves in a small pan until warm and golden, but not browned.

8 When all the pasta is in the serving dish, pour over the melted butter and mix carefully to distribute. Sprinkle with the remaining Parmesan cheese and serve immediately.

COOK'S TIP

Any scraps of dough can be finely chopped and set aside to dry. They can be used in a clear broth to make a simple soup.

PER PORTION Energy 616kcal/2579kJ; Protein 28g; Carbohydrate 27g, of which sugars 2g; Fat 44g, of which saturates 26g; Cholesterol 350mg; Calcium 505mg; Fibre 0.7g; Sodium 379mg.

ANCHOVY AND WHITE FISH RAVIOLI

RAVIOLI RIPIENI DI PESCE

Anchovies and tomato purée, combined with white fish, make this a really special dish with an intense flavour, from Emilia-Romagna. The fragrant herb butter is the only dressing for these ravioli, complementing and not overpowering them.

SERVES 6

4 canned anchovy fillets, drained
a little milk
45ml/3 tbsp olive oil
1 onion, finely chopped
2 celery sticks, chopped
1 carrot, finely chopped
2 garlic cloves, chopped
45ml/3 tbsp chopped flat leaf parsley
60ml/4 tbsp tomato purée (paste), diluted in 45ml/3 tbsp hot water
350g/12oz white fish fillets, such as cod, haddock, hake, plaice or flounder, boned and skinned
sea salt and ground black pepper

FOR THE PASTA

200g/7oz/1¾ cups plain (all-purpose) flour
200g/7oz/generous 1 cup fine semolina
4 whole eggs

TO SERVE

300g/11oz/generous 1½ cups unsalted butter, melted
finely chopped parsley, chervil and a little tarragon

1 Soak the anchovies in just enough milk to cover for 30 minutes, then rinse and dry on kitchen paper.

2 Heat the olive oil in a pan and add the anchovy fillets. Mash the anchovies to a pulp, using a fork, then add the onion, celery, carrot, garlic and parsley. Mix together and fry gently together for 10 minutes, or until soft.

3 Add the diluted tomato purée and simmer for 15 minutes. Add the fish. Mix again and cook until a thick sauce is formed and the fish has broken up. Season to taste, then take off the heat and set aside to cool completely.

4 To make the pasta, pile the flour and semolina on to the work surface and make a hollow in the centre with your fist. Break the eggs into a bowl and whisk together briefly. Pour into the hollow in the flour.

5 Using your fingers, mix the eggs roughly into the flour, then use both your hands to knead everything together thoroughly until you have a smooth, pliable ball of dough. Wrap the dough in clear film (plastic wrap) and leave to rest for 20 minutes.

6 Roll the dough out as thinly as possible using a pasta machine or a rolling pin. Cut the dough into two even sheets.

7 Lay out one sheet of dough on the table and dot teaspoonfuls of the filling along the sheet in evenly spaced rows.

8 Lay the second sheet of dough on top and press around each covered mound of filling with the sides of your hands to press out all the air. Cut around each mound with a ravioli cutter or pastry (cookie) cutter. They can be square or round, or even triangular. Leave them to dry until required.

9 Bring a large pan of salted water to a gentle boil. Drop in the ravioli and cook, in batches, for 3–4 minutes, or until they are floating on top of the water. Drain and transfer to a warmed serving dish. Serve immediately, with the melted butter spooned over and sprinkled with the chopped herbs.

COOK'S TIP

Work fast while making the ravioli to prevent the sheets of dough from drying out. Keep the dough pliable at all times.

PER PORTION Energy 425kcal/1791kJ; Protein 24g; Carbohydrate 55g, of which sugars 3g; Fat 14g, of which saturates 3g; Cholesterol 183mg; Calcium 104mg; Fibre 2.7g; Sodium 210mg.

TORTELLINI IN BROTH
TORTELLINI IN BRODO

This very traditional dish is served on Christmas Eve, often after midnight Mass in many households of northern Italy. It is normal practice in Italy to ask people whether they would prefer their tortellini with more or less brodo and to serve it accordingly.

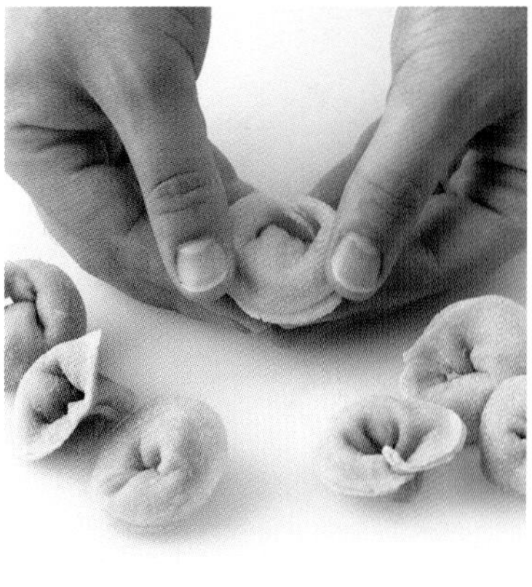

SERVES 10

350g/12oz/3 cups plain (all-purpose) flour
350g/12oz/2 cups fine semolina
7 eggs, beaten
freshly grated Parmesan cheese, to serve

FOR THE BRODO

1 large boiling fowl or capon
3 carrots, trimmed
3 onions, halved
2 celery sticks, halved
2 tomatoes, halved
2 cabbage leaves
25g/1oz parsley
4 litres/7 pints/17 cups cold water
sea salt

FOR THE FILLING

50g/2oz/$\frac{1}{4}$ cup unsalted butter
100g/$3\frac{3}{4}$oz pork loin, cubed
50g/2oz turkey breast, cubed
100g/$3\frac{3}{4}$oz mortadella, in one piece
115g/4oz prosciutto crudo, in one piece (preferably prosciutto di Parma)
2 eggs, beaten
175g/6oz/2 cups freshly grated Parmesan cheese
large pinch of grated nutmeg
sea salt and ground black pepper

1 To make the brodo, put the bird in a large pan with the vegetables and parsley, and a little salt. Bring to the boil slowly and leave to simmer gently for about 2 hours. Leave to cool in the pan.

2 Remove the bird and reserve for another meal (see Cook's Tips). Strain the liquid through a fine sieve (strainer). Leave to stand, remove any fat that forms and strain again. You will need 3 litres/5 pints/$12\frac{1}{2}$ cups.

3 To make the filling, melt the butter in a frying pan, add the the pork and turkey, and fry for 10 minutes, until cooked through. Mince the meat three times using a hand mincer, or process once in a food processor, together with the mortadella and prosciutto. Stir in the 2 eggs, Parmesan cheese, nutmeg and seasoning. Mix together thoroughly and set aside.

4 Pile the flour and semolina on a work surface and make a hollow in the centre with your fist. Pour in the 7 beaten eggs. Using your fingers, mix the eggs roughly into the flour, then use both hands to knead everything together until you have a smooth, pliable ball of dough. Rest the dough under a clean cloth or wrap in clear film (plastic wrap) for 20 minutes.

5 Roll out the pasta very thinly using a pasta machine or rolling pin. Lay the sheet of pasta carefully on to a very lightly floured surface. You must work quickly to prevent it drying out.

6 Cut the dough into circles using a 4cm/$1\frac{1}{2}$in pastry (cookie) cutter. Put 1.5ml/$\frac{1}{4}$ tsp of filling in the centre. Fold in half and hold between your middle and index finger. Wrap the two extremities around the tip of your index finger. Push the filled pasta pocket off your finger and turn it half inside out so that it looks like a little belly button. Press the ends together.

7 Bring the brodo to a very gentle boil and add the tortellini. Simmer for 8 minutes, or until the tortellini are cooked and float, then remove from the heat.

8 Ladle the soup into individual bowls and serve, sprinkled with Parmesan cheese.

COOK'S TIPS

- You can open freeze fresh pasta on trays, then transfer them to bags and freeze for up to 1 month.
- You can use the cooked boiling fowl for another meal, if you like. It is good for slicing for sandwiches or making a tasty salad.

PER PORTION Energy 752kcal/3151kJ; Protein 48g; Carbohydrate 61g, of which sugars 6g; Fat 37g, of which saturates 14g; Cholesterol 353mg; Calcium 306mg; Fibre 3.5g; Sodium 619mg.

CLASSIC RAGÙ BOLOGNESE
RAGÙ CLASSICO ALLA BOLOGNESE

A combination of several different kinds of meat, chopped with a heavy knife, are fundamental to this version of a classic pasta sauce which uses only a tiny amount of tomato purée to give it sweetness and colour. Long cooking time over a very low heat is essential and this is one sauce that improves after being left for a day and then reheating. Serve it with tagliatelle for a truly authentic Ragù Bolognese.

1 Chop the meats together using a heavy knife. Melt half the butter in a frying pan and fry the vegetables and pancetta or bacon for 5–6 minutes, stirring. Add the meats and stir together to seal all over.

2 Add the diluted tomato purée and season with salt and pepper. Stir thoroughly, then cover and leave to simmer very slowly for 2 hours, stirring frequently, until tender. Add a little hot water or broth as necessary to keep it moist.

3 Add the chopped chicken livers to the pan and simmer for 5 minutes, then stir in the cream, and the truffle, if using.

4 Leave the ragù to stand until required. You can, of course, use it immediately, but it does improve with standing and reheating.

5 Serve the ragù with tagliatelle, cooked according to the packet instructions until al dente. Sprinkle with Parmesan cheese.

SERVES 4

115g/4oz pork loin, boned
115g/4oz beef steak, boned (rib-eye preferably)
115g/4oz prosciutto crudo
115g/4oz/½ cup unsalted butter
1 carrot, finely chopped
1 celery stick, finely chopped
1 onion, finely chopped
50g/2oz pancetta or streaky (fatty) bacon, finely chopped
25ml/1½ tbsp tomato purée (paste), diluted in 175ml/6fl oz/¾ cup hot water
175ml/6fl oz/¾ cup hot broth or water
115g/4oz chicken livers, trimmed and finely chopped
90ml/6 tbsp double (heavy) or single (light) cream
1 small truffle, cleaned and thinly sliced (optional)
sea salt and ground black pepper
tagliatelle and freshly grated Parmesan cheese, to serve

PER PORTION Energy 584kcal/2433kJ; Protein 28g; Carbohydrate 6g, of which sugars 5g; Fat 50g, of which saturates 28g; Cholesterol 249mg; Calcium 42mg; Fibre 1.3g; Sodium 821mg.

SERVES 4

75g/3oz/6 tbsp unsalted butter
1 onion, chopped
1 celery stick, chopped
400g/14oz boned chicken, cubed
juice and grated rind of 1/2 lemon, plus extra grated rind, to garnish
250ml/8fl oz/1 cup dry white wine
250ml/8fl oz/1 cup chicken stock, plus extra if needed
400g/14oz garganelli
10ml/2 tsp chopped parsley
175ml/6fl oz/3/4 cup double (heavy) cream
sea salt and ground black pepper
freshly grated Parmesan cheese, to serve

PER PORTION Energy 869kcal/3654kJ; Protein 36g; Carbohydrate 80g, of which sugars 6g; Fat 43g, of which saturates 26g; Cholesterol 193mg; Calcium 76mg; Fibre 3.8g; Sodium 282mg.

WHITE RAGÙ WITH GARGANELLI
RAGÙ BIANCO CON GARGANELLI

Any white meat will work for this recipe, so turkey, rabbit or veal can all be used instead of chicken. Lamb can also be used, but the result is a totally different dish. The 'white' in the recipe title actually refers to the fact that no tomato is used for this. Garganelli are a kind of handmade egg pasta shape, similar to penne, which are dried until hard. They are a speciality from Bologna. Normal dried penne or maccheroni, or even fresh tagliatelle, will also work well with this sauce.

1 Heat half the butter in a frying pan, add the onion and celery, and fry together gently for 5 minutes, or until soft.

2 Add the chicken and cook, stirring, to brown the meat gently all over. Add the lemon rind and juice. Stir together and add the white wine.

3 Boil hard for 1–2 minutes to evaporate the alcohol, and then reduce the heat.

4 Add the chicken stock, season and simmer, stirring frequently and adding extra stock if necessary, for 1 hour, until the meat is tender.

5 Meanwhile, cook the pasta in salted boiling water according to the packet instructions.

6 Take the sauce off the heat and stir in the remaining butter, the parsley and cream. Stir in the garganelli and serve, sprinkled with Parmesan cheese and lemon rind.

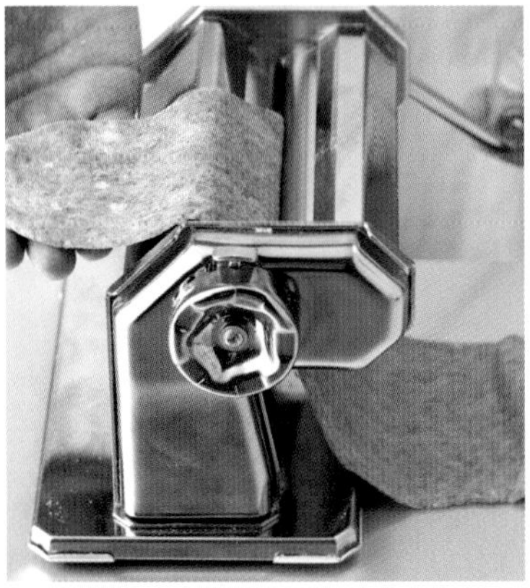

LASAGNA IN THE FERRARA STYLE

LASAGNA ALLA FERRARESE

This traditional lasagna recipe from the city of Ferrara uses lots of ingredients and a very specific way of making the basic ragù. It is usually saved for special occasions.

SERVES 6 TO 8

300g/11oz spinach, rinsed
200g/7oz/1¾ cups plain (all-purpose) flour
200g/7oz/generous 1 cup fine semolina
4 eggs, beaten
5ml/1 tsp olive oil
freshly grated Parmesan cheese, to serve

FOR THE RAGÙ

130g/4½oz/9 tbsp unsalted butter
115g/4oz pancetta, cubed
1 large carrot, finely chopped
1 large onion, finely chopped
2 celery sticks, finely chopped
200g/7oz pork loin, roughly chopped
200g/7oz beef steak (preferably rib-eye), roughly chopped
200g/7oz prosciutto crudo, chopped
60ml/4 tbsp tomato purée (paste), stirred into 250ml/8fl oz/1 cup beef stock
250ml/8fl oz/1 cup dry red wine
115g/4oz peas, cooked
115g/4oz chicken livers, trimmed
90ml/6 tbsp double (heavy) cream
sea salt and ground black pepper

FOR THE WHITE SAUCE

115g/4oz/½ cup unsalted butter
115g/4oz/1 cup plain (all-purpose) flour
1 litre/1¾ pints/4 cups milk, warmed
pinch of salt
pinch of grated nutmeg
150g/5oz/1½ cups freshly grated Parmesan cheese

1 To make the ragù, heat 115g/4oz/½ cup butter in a frying pan and fry the pancetta, carrot, onion and celery together until the vegetables are all softened. Add the pork, beef and prosciutto and cook until browned. Add the tomato purée and stock mixture and stir, then add the wine. Boil for 1 minute, to evaporate the alcohol, then add the peas, season and reduce the heat. Cover and simmer for 1 hour, then remove from the heat.

2 Meanwhile, make the pasta. Put the rinsed spinach in a pan with just the water that clings to the leaves, cover and cook for 2 minutes. Drain. Squeeze the spinach as dry as possible. Chop or process to a purée.

3 Pile the flour and semolina on to the work surface and blend them together with your fingers. Make a hollow in the centre with your fist and pour in the beaten eggs. Add the spinach and work the flour, spinach and eggs to make a smooth, elastic dough. Wrap it in clear film (plastic wrap) and leave it to rest for 20 minutes.

4 While the dough is resting, make the white sauce. Melt the butter in a pan until foaming, add the flour and mix to a roux. Add the milk and whisk vigorously. Add salt and nutmeg. Simmer, stirring frequently, until smooth. Remove from the heat, stir in half the Parmesan, then cover the surface with a little cold water to prevent a skin forming.

5 Take apple-sized balls of dough and work them through a pasta machine from the widest setting to the narrowest. Alternatively, roll it out with a rolling pin as thinly as possible. Cut it into 7.5 x 15cm/3 x 6in rectangles.

6 Cook the lasagna sheets, four at a time, in a pan of salted boiling water for 1 minute. Remove with a slotted spoon and drop into a bowl of cold water with the olive oil, to keep them soft and stop them sticking together.

7 In a separate pan, fry the chicken livers in the rest of the butter until sealed and browned. Stir them into the ragù. Heat the ragù to a simmer, stir in the cream, then remove from the heat. Preheat the oven to 180°C/350°F/Gas 4.

8 Cover the base of a large, shallow ovenproof dish with a little white sauce, then add a layer of blotted lasagna sheets. Add a layer of ragù, followed by a little Parmesan. Repeat with the remaining ingredients, finishing with white sauce and Parmesan. Bake for 30–40 minutes. Rest for 5 minutes before serving, sprinkled with extra Parmesan.

PER PORTION Energy 953kcal/3996kJ; Protein 46g; Carbohydrate 62g, of which sugars 11g; Fat 57g, of which saturates 31g; Cholesterol 320mg; Calcium 521mg; Fibre 4.2g; Sodium 1051mg.

SERVES 6

1kg/2¼lb floury potatoes, scrubbed
3 eggs, beaten
about 300g/11oz/2⅔ cups plain (all-purpose) flour
185g/6½oz Gorgonzola cheese
400ml/14fl oz/1⅔ cups milk
about 105ml/7 tbsp sunflower oil
about 30 sage leaves
butter, for greasing
salt
freshly grated Parmesan cheese, to serve (optional)

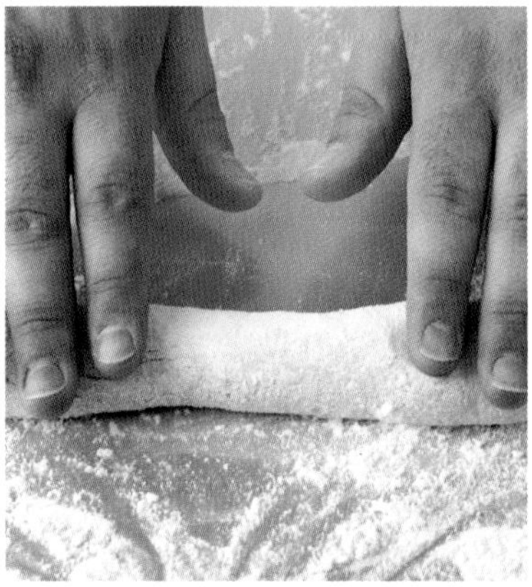

GNOCCHI WITH GORGONZOLA
GNOCCHI AL GORGONZOLA

This is the ultimate cold weather dish, comforting, rich, sublimely tasty and very hearty! Gorgonzola comes in two varieties: 'dolce', which is gentle and creamy or 'piccante' which is slightly drier and salty. Either can be used in this dish.

1 Boil the potatoes until soft, then drain and peel quickly. Press through a potato ricer, mouli or a wide-meshed sieve (strainer) twice. Blend in the eggs.

2 Working carefully and quickly, gradually add just enough flour for the mixture to hold its shape, handling it as little as possible. Form a soft dough with your hands, then roll it all into long thumb-thick cylinders.

3 Cut the cylinders into 2.5cm/1in sections (you should make about 72) and form into small concave gnocchi shapes by pressing them against the back of a fork or a flat cheese grater. Spread them out on large board and set aside until required.

4 Put the Gorgonzola cheese and the milk into a bowl and set it over a pan of simmering water. Stir together gently so that the milk does not curdle (which will make the sauce granular), until the cheese melts into the milk.

5 Bring a large pan of salted water to the boil, drop in the gnocchi and allow them to cook until they float on the surface. This should take about 1 minute if the gnocchi are really light.

6 While the gnocchi are cooking, heat the sunflower oil in a pan until sizzling and fry the sage leaves for 20 seconds or until crisp. Drain the leaves on kitchen paper and set aside until required.

7 Scoop out the gnocchi with a slotted spoon and arrange them in a warm, well-buttered ovenproof dish. You need about 12 gnocchi per person.

8 Dress the drained gnocchi with the melted Gorgonzola cheese as soon as they come out of the pan, and toss together very gently.

9 Garnish with a few fried sage leaves to serve. Offer freshly grated Parmesan cheese separately at the table, if you like.

COOK'S TIPS

- The amount of flour you'll need will depend on the texture of the potatoes.
- The gnocchi must not be made in a food processor as the texture will be too heavy.

PER PORTION Energy 646kcal/2705kJ; Protein 20g; Carbohydrate 71g, of which sugars 5g; Fat 33g, of which saturates 10g; Cholesterol 148mg; Calcium 350mg; Fibre 3.7g; Sodium 600mg.

GREEN AND YELLOW POLENTA MOULD
SFORMATO DI POLENTA VERDE E GIALLA

This is a very different way of serving both polenta and ragù, put together in a pretty combination to make a rather sturdy dish. You can of course fill the centre of the mould with a cheesy sauce or mushrooms instead of the ragù.

SERVES 8

400g/14oz yellow polenta flour
200g/7oz cooked spinach, drained and puréed
40g/1½oz/½ cup freshly grated Parmesan cheese, plus extra to serve
butter, for greasing
2 x quantity of Classic Ragù Bolognese (see page 50)
sea salt

1 First prepare the polenta. Bring 3 litres/5 pints/12½ cups water to the boil, add a pinch of salt and reduce it to a simmer.

2 Drizzle in the polenta flour initially whisking, then, as it thickens, stirring constantly. Note that quick-cook polenta will take only a few minutes, whereas the traditional variety will need close to an hour to cook.

3 When the polenta is cooked, transfer half of it into a large bowl. Add the puréed spinach and half of the Parmesan to one half. Stir the remaining Parmesan into the other half.

4 Grease a 3-litre/5-pint ring mould with butter. Preheat the oven to 200°C/400°F/Gas 6.

5 Fill the bottom of the mould with the yellow polenta, pressing it down firmly. It should come about halfway up the sides. Add the green polenta, pressing it down firmly and banging the mould gently on the work surface to ensure there are no air pockets.

6 Gently reheat the ragù, if necessary, until bubbling hot.

7 Cook the filled mould in the hot oven for about 10 minutes to heat through, then remove from the oven and turn it out on to a platter.

8 Pour the hot ragù into the the centre and serve immediately, sprinkled with Parmesan.

PER PORTION Energy 793kcal/3309kJ; Protein 35g; Carbohydrate 43g, of which sugars 5g; Fat 53g, of which saturates 29g; Cholesterol 253mg; Calcium 135mg; Fibre 2.9g; Sodium 889mg.

CLASSIC MILANESE RISOTTO
RISOTTO ALLA MILANESE CLASSICO

The origins of this classic dish belong to an Italian legend about the chief stained-glass-window master of Milan Cathedral, who employed a keen workman to paint the yellow robes of St Helen. The workman used saffron to colour the glass and he was so passionate about his saffron powder that he was named Zafferano (meaning 'saffron') by his colleagues, who claimed that one day he'd probably even add it to his risotto! And one day he did: on the occasion of the wedding of the master's daughter, he presented two tureens of the golden risotto, coloured and scented with saffron as a gift. This traditional recipe includes beef bone marrow but, if you prefer, use only butter instead.

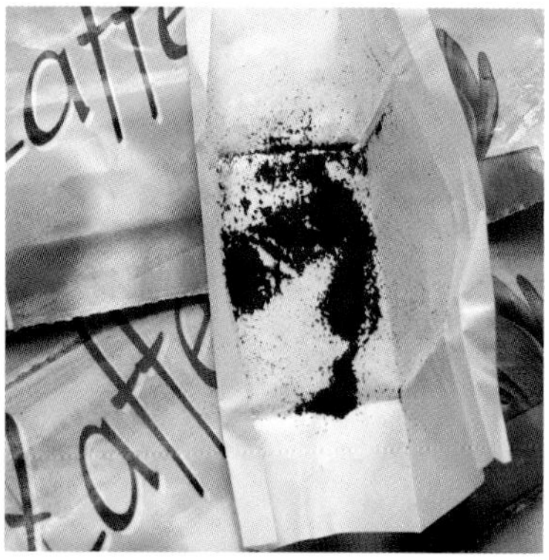

1 Soak the onion in cold water for 10 minutes, then drain and squeeze dry in a napkin.

2 Heat half the butter in a pan, add the onion and fry very slowly with the beef marrow, if using, for 5 minutes, or until soft. Add the rice. Stir and coat the grains thoroughly until the rice grains are crackling hot but not coloured.

3 Add a ladleful of the stock and stir constantly, allowing the liquid to be absorbed into the rice. Add another ladleful of stock and continue in this way, making sure that the rice always absorbs the stock before you add more.

4 After 10 minutes of cooking time, add the saffron powder and stir through. Continue cooking the risotto, adding stock a ladleful at a time, and stirring constantly. The risotto will take about 20 minutes to cook: when it is creamy and velvety, but the rice grains are still firm to the bite, take it off the heat.

5 Stir in the remaining butter and the cheese. Cover and leave to rest for 2 minutes, then stir again and transfer to a warmed platter. Serve immediately, offering extra grated Parmesan cheese at the table, to sprinkle on top.

SERVES 6

$\frac{1}{2}$ onion, finely chopped
115g/4oz/$\frac{1}{2}$ cup unsalted butter
40g/$1\frac{1}{2}$oz raw beef bone marrow, chopped (optional)
500g/$1\frac{1}{4}$lb vialone gigante, or other risotto rice
1.5 litres/$2\frac{1}{2}$ pints/$6\frac{1}{4}$ cups hot rich veal, beef, chicken or vegetable stock
1–2 sachets of saffron powder
50g/2oz/$\frac{2}{3}$ cup freshly grated Parmesan cheese, plus extra to serve

PER PORTION Energy 484kcal/2023kJ; Protein 10g; Carbohydrate 64g, of which sugars 1g; Fat 20g, of which saturates 12g; Cholesterol 52mg; Calcium 105mg; Fibre 0.2g; Sodium 763mg.

SERVES 6

2 litres/3½ pints/9 cups good-quality beef or veal stock
500g/1¼lb carnaroli rice
65g/2½oz/¾ cup freshly grated Parmesan cheese
65g/2½oz/5 tbsp unsalted butter
65g/2½oz finely sliced black or white truffle
pinch of grated nutmeg
sea salt
shavings of Parmesan cheese and black or white truffle, to serve

PER PORTION Energy 430kcal/1979kJ; Protein 11g; Carbohydrate 63g, of which sugars 1g; Fat 14g, of which saturates 8g; Cholesterol 35mg; Calcium 127mg; Fibre 0.1g; Sodium 1013mg.

PIEDMONTESE RISOTTO
RISOTTO ALLA PIEMONTESE

This recipe is all about the luxurious truffle: the more the better! The other vital ingredient is, of course, the stock. This is particularly important because this is a very old risotto recipe and the rice is effectively gently boiled and then dressed, rather than being toasted before the stock is gradually added, until the rice is cooked and creamy. Unlike most risottos, the Piedmontese risotto is very wet in consistency and served almost like a soup.

1 Bring the stock to a gentle boil in a large pan. Add the rice and stir. Simmer until tender, stirring occasionally for about 20 minutes. This risotto should be quite soupy and wet. Remove from the heat.

2 Add the Parmesan cheese, butter, truffle and nutmeg. Taste and adjust the seasoning. Cover and rest for 4 minutes, then stir again and serve in deep soup plates or bowls, with Parmesan and truffle shavings on top.

BAROLO RISOTTO
RISOTTO AL BAROLO

This is a very old recipe for making a traditional Piedmontese dish. Although it is more complicated than some of the more modern versions of similar risotto dishes, the end result is utterly delicious and hugely filling and satisfying, containing not just the rice and the wine, but also beans, meat and vegetables. Barolo is a rather expensive but wonderful wine, and imparts intense flavour in this dish. The borlotti beans will need to be soaked overnight whether they are dried or fresh.

SERVES 6

200g/7oz fresh or dried borlotti beans, soaked overnight
300g/11oz stewing veal
1 onion, whole and 1 onion, finely chopped
1 celery stick
1 carrot
115g/4oz/$^{1}/_{2}$ cup unsalted butter
500g/1$^{1}/_{4}$lb/scant 3 cups risotto rice
750ml/1$^{1}/_{4}$ pints/3 cups Barolo wine
90g/3$^{1}/_{2}$oz/generous 1 cup freshly grated Parmesan cheese, plus extra to serve
sea salt and ground black pepper

1 Drain and rinse the beans, then cover with water and bring to the boil. Boil hard for 5 minutes. Drain again, then cover with water and simmer gently until tender. (Do not add salt, as it will make the skins toughen.) Strain the beans and set aside until required.

2 Put the stewing veal into a large pan with the whole onion, the celery and the carrot. Cover with 1.2 litres/2 pints/5 cups cold water, add a little salt and boil slowly for 2 hours, skimming occasionally.

3 Remove the meat and the vegetables from the pan. Trim the meat, then chop the meat and vegetables finely. Set them aside and strain the stock into a clean pan. Adjust the seasoning to taste, bring to the boil and allow to simmer.

4 Heat half the butter in a large, heavy pan. Fry the chopped onion gently for about 5 minutes, until soft and golden. Add all the rice and toast it quickly in the hot butter and onion. When it is well coated, shiny and hot, add about 175ml/6fl oz/$^{3}/_{4}$ cup Barolo.

5 Stir the rice and allow the alcohol to evaporate, then add a ladleful of hot stock. Stir and allow the rice to absorb the liquid, then add another 175ml/6fl oz/$^{3}/_{4}$ cup Barolo. Continue in this way, adding wine and stock alternately and stirring in between each addition, until the rice is half cooked. This should take about 10 minutes. Add salt and pepper to taste, then add the beans with more wine and stock.

6 Cook for a further 4 minutes, then add the chopped meat and vegetables. Continue as before until the risotto is creamy and velvety, but the rice grains are still firm to the bite: it should take about 20 minutes to cook. Remove from the heat.

7 Add the remaining butter and the Parmesan cheese. Stir together thoroughly, then cover with a lid and leave to stand for 5 minutes before serving, sprinkled with extra Parmesan cheese.

COOK'S TIP

You can use a 400g/14oz can of borlotti beans, drained, rather than fresh or dried, if you prefer.

PER PORTION Energy 772kcal/3237kJ; Protein 32g; Carbohydrate 87g, of which sugars 5g; Fat 23g, of which saturates 14g; Cholesterol 84mg; Calcium 244mg; Fibre 1.1g; Sodium 164mg.

FISH AND SHELLFISH
PESCE E FRUTTI DI MARE

With no coastline, Lombardy, Piedmont and the Aosta Valley rely on fish from the lakes rather than from the sea for their traditional fish dishes, though fish and shellfish are transported to the local markets from other parts of the country. The fish dishes created around the lakes Garda, Maggiore, Iseo and Como tend to be prepared very simply. Liguria and Emilia-Romagna have easier access to the sea, and their fish and shellfish dishes are more plentiful, though not as much as you might imagine: it is said that the seafaring men of Liguria had to eat so much fish while on their voyages that the last thing they wanted when they came home was yet more fish! Saying that, there are several delectable Ligurian fish dishes that make use of the fragrant olive oil, combining it with herbs and pine nuts to create recipes that show off the taste of fresh fish to its full glory.

PROSCIUTTO-WRAPPED FISH AND SMOOTH FISH SOUP

Emilia-Romagna is divided when it comes to cooking with fish: the region spreads from the Adriatic right up to the mountains of Piedmont, so there are great variations in culinary culture. The two historical regions, Emilia and Romagna, which make up present-day Emilia-Romagna, are quite distinct. Romagna celebrates fish and shellfish along its coastline, with eels being a favourite in the town of Comacchio and its surroundings. In Romagna there is an ancient tradition of cooking fish on terracotta tiles. Traditionally, there are few fish dishes in the cuisine of Emilia due to its lack of coastline. Emilian cooking relies much more on cured meats as well as flavoursome Parmesan cheese, which is not surprising given that it contains the city of Parma.

Liguria, with its long coastline, has a small selection of lovely fish dishes, the most famous and extravagant of which is called cappon magro. This labour-intensive recipe is still used today for those who wish to prepare the original dish, which is Genoa's traditional Christmas Eve dinner specialty. It can be tasted in some special Ligurian restaurants, though it usually must be reserved in advance. It contains lobster, anchovies, oysters, shrimp, sea bass, dried fish roe and a huge selection of vegetables and herbs, all of which make it unmistakably Ligurian. Less extravagant dishes include a wonderful soup, ciuppin, which is served with slices of ciabatta in the bowl.

The mountainous Piedmont, Aosta Valley and Lombardy have historically tended to use freshwater fish, such as tench or carp, from the lakes, though easy transportation of fresh sea-water fish and shellfish now allows them to be included on the local menus.

PINOT

SMOOTH LIGURIAN FISH SOUP
CIUPPIN

This is the easiest recipe for making a truly Italian-tasting velvety smooth fish soup. You can add whole cooked mussels or prawns (shrimp) at the end if you wish, although the basic recipe as it appears here calls only for whole fish. The bread soaks up all the flavours and juices of the fish and is eaten at the end, once all the soup has been enjoyed. A lot of the flavour comes from the crushed bones of the fish, but you could bone the fish before using, if you prefer.

1 Heat the oil in a large, deep pan, add the finely chopped garlic, parsley and tomatoes, and cook for 5 minutes.

2 Add all the fish and stir. Season with salt and pepper and pour over the fish stock.

3 Cover tightly with a lid and simmer very gently for 25 minutes.

4 Remove from the heat and cool slightly, then pass through a sieve (strainer) or food mill. Return to the heat for about 10 minutes, until reduced and thickened a little.

5 Rub the toasted bread with the whole garlic and place two slices in each bowl. Pour the soup over the bread and serve immediately, sprinkled with chopped parsley.

SERVES 6

120ml/4fl oz/$^1/_2$ cup olive oil
4 garlic cloves, finely chopped, and 1 garlic clove, peeled and left whole
60ml/4 tbsp chopped fresh parsley
8 cherry tomatoes
1.5kg/3$^1/_4$lb whole fish, such as cod, monkfish, haddock, plaice or flounder, cleaned
about 200ml/7fl oz/scant 1 cup fish stock
12 slices ciabatta bread, toasted
sea salt and ground black pepper
30ml/2 tbsp chopped fresh parsley, to garnish

PER PORTION Energy 477kcal/2005kJ; Protein 33g; Carbohydrate 36g, of which sugars 3g; Fat 23g, of which saturates 3g; Cholesterol 23mg; Calcium 103mg; Fibre 2g; Sodium 485mg.

SERVES 8

plain (all-purpose) flour, for dusting
2kg/4½lb firm fish fillet, such as haddock, cod, hake or monkfish
105ml/7 tbsp sunflower oil
30ml/2 tbsp olive oil
1 lemon, sliced

FOR THE MARINADE

75ml/5 tbsp olive oil
4 onions, sliced
2 garlic cloves, crushed
1 fresh rosemary sprig
1 fresh parsley sprig
about 8 sage leaves
90ml/6 tbsp white wine vinegar
sea salt

PER PORTION Energy 470kcal/1956kJ; Protein 47g; Carbohydrate 7g, of which sugars 4g; Fat 28g, of which saturates 4g; Cholesterol 115mg; Calcium 43mg; Fibre 1.1g; Sodium 153mg.

FISH IN CARPIONE

PESCE IN CARPIONE

From Lombardy comes this method of serving fish, which would traditionally have been made with freshwater fish, such as tench or carp, from the lakes. This recipe, however, uses firm sea fish fillets. Start preparations the day before.

1 Put the flour on a plate or in a plastic bag, mix in a pinch of salt and use to dust the fish all over.

2 Heat the sunflower oil and olive oil in a frying pan over a low heat and sauté the fish for 4 minutes on each side. Remove with a slotted spoon and place on kitchen paper to soak up the excess oil, then arrange in a dish. Cover with slices of lemon.

3 To make the marinade, heat the olive oil in a small pan over a medium heat, then add the onions, garlic and herbs. Cook for 5 minutes, or until the onions are soft but not browned.

4 Add the vinegar, raise the heat and reduce slightly. Remove from the heat, cool completely and then pour over the fish fillets. Place in the refrigerator to marinate for 24 hours before serving.

SERVES 4

1 trout, about 1kg/2¼lb, cleaned and left whole
60ml/4 tbsp extra virgin olive oil
500ml/17fl oz/2¼ cups dry white wine
2 garlic cloves (1 left whole, and 1 crushed)
300ml/½ pint/1¼ cups passata (bottled strained tomatoes)
45ml/3 tbsp chopped parsley
sea salt and ground black pepper
5ml/1 tsp dried oregano, to garnish

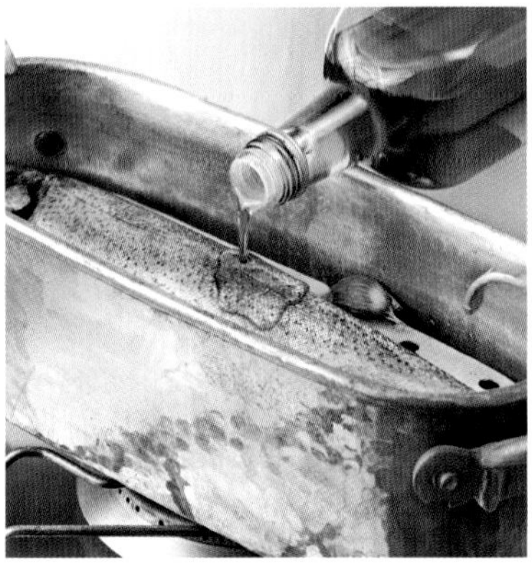

TROUT DOGANA STYLE
TROTA ALLA DOGANA

On the outskirts of the town of Sirmione is an old building that was once an Austrian barracks from the days of the Hapsburg Empire. It later became the Ristorante Dogana and is famous all over the area for its simple cuisine, as epitomized by this trout dish.

1 Rinse the cavity of the trout and pat it dry, then place in a fish kettle. Add the oil, wine, whole garlic clove, 250ml/8fl oz/1 cup cold water, and salt and pepper, then set over a high heat and bring to the boil. Reduce the heat and cook the fish very gently for 30–40 minutes.

2 Carefully lift out the fish and transfer to an ovenproof serving dish.

3 Preheat the oven to 200°C/400°F/Gas 6. Put the passata into a small pan and simmer for 5 minutes with the crushed garlic, parsley, and salt and pepper to taste. Keep warm.

4 Pour the tomato sauce over the fish, and place in the oven for 2–3 minutes, until heated through. Sprinkle lightly with oregano and serve, with roast potatoes, if you like.

PER PORTION Energy 420kcal/1751kJ; Protein 30g; Carbohydrate 3g, of which sugars 3g; Fat 23g, of which saturates 4g; Cholesterol 101mg; Calcium 56mg; Fibre 0.7g; Sodium 103mg.

SEA BREAM WITH PINE KERNELS AND OLIVES

ORATA CON PINOLI E OLIVE

In this flavoursome recipe from Liguria, succulent sea bream is baked on a bed of potatoes, olives and pine nuts. It is made with Taggiasca olives, which are grown in Liguria. However, if you cannot find them, you can use any other black olives instead.

SERVES 4 TO 6

400g/14oz potatoes, peeled
2kg/4½lb sea bream, cleaned and small bones removed
1 sprig each of fresh rosemary, thyme and sage
90ml/6 tbsp extra virgin olive oil
25g/1oz pine nuts
175g/6oz Taggiasca olives
300ml/½ pint/1¼ cups dry white wine
sea salt

1 Preheat the oven to 180°C/350°F/Gas 4. Parboil the potatoes for 8 minutes, then drain and slice thinly. Meanwhile, season the fish inside and add the fresh herb sprigs.

2 Grease an ovenproof dish large enough to take the fish with a little of the oil. Create a flat layer in the base of the dish using the potatoes, pine nuts and olives.

3 Lay the fish on top of the potatoes, pine nuts and olives and drizzle with the remaining oil.

4 Put the dish into the oven and cook for about 10 minutes, or until the oil begins to sizzle, then remove from the oven and pour the wine around the fish. Return to the oven and continue cooking for a further 20 minutes, or until the fish is cooked through.

PER PORTION Energy 373kcal/1550kJ; Protein 20g; Carbohydrate 12g, of which sugars 1g; Fat 24g, of which saturates 3g; Cholesterol 38mg; Calcium 66mg; Fibre 1.8g; Sodium 773mg.

GENOESE TUNA
TONNO ALLA GENOVESE

The combination of tuna and mushrooms is quite unusual, but in this lovely light dish from Genoa, made with wild mushrooms picked in the woody hinterland, the two ingredients come together perfectly. The result is great with roasted cherry tomatoes.

1 Put the tuna steaks in a large shallow dish or bowl, and add the chopped onion and garlic, half the chopped parsley, and 90ml/6 tbsp olive oil. Season with plenty of ground black pepper.

2 Add about one-third of the wine and cover with clear film (plastic wrap). Leave to marinate in the refrigerator for about 3 hours.

3 Clean the mushrooms using a brush or a slightly damp cloth. Trim and slice them thinly.

4 Heat the remaining olive oil in a large frying pan, add the mushrooms and cook over a medium heat for 4–5 minutes until all the excess liquid from the mushrooms has evaporated. Season the mushrooms with salt and ground pepper, then remove the pan from the heat.

5 Drain the tuna steaks from the marinade and blot them with kitchen paper. Put the pan with the mushrooms back on the heat, add the tuna steaks and the remaining white wine.

6 Cook the tuna steaks quickly over a high heat for 3 minutes on each side – the alcohol will evaporate during this quick cooking process. Remove the pan from the heat.

7 Season with salt and ground black pepper, then sprinkle over the remaining parsley. Serve immediately with lemon wedges and roasted whole cherry tomatoes, if you like.

SERVES 4

4 tuna steaks, about 600g/1lb 6oz total weight
1 small onion, finely chopped
1 large garlic clove, chopped
45ml/3 tbsp chopped fresh flat leaf parsley
135ml/9 tbsp extra virgin olive oil
175ml/6fl oz/¾ cup dry white wine
300g/11oz wild mushrooms
sea salt and ground black pepper
lemon wedges, to serve
roasted whole cherry tomatoes, to serve (optional, see Cook's Tip)

COOK'S TIP

To roast cherry tomatoes, preheat the oven to 200°C/400°F/Gas 6 and line a baking sheet with foil. Place the tomatoes on the baking sheet (you can leave them on the vine), drizzle with olive oil and sprinkle with a little salt. Cook for 10 minutes.

PER PORTION Energy 553kcal/2298kJ; Protein 37g; Carbohydrate 2g, of which sugars 1g; Fat 41g, of which saturates 7g; Cholesterol 42mg; Calcium 41mg; Fibre 1.2g; Sodium 77mg.

POACHED SEA BASS IN THE ROMAGNOLA STYLE
BRANZINO LESSO ALLA ROMAGNOLA

As with all fish dishes, the real key to success is the absolute freshness of the fish, so that it can be cooked, dressed and served as simply as possible. You an use this method for other whole fish, such as a bream, or even freshwater fish, such as trout.

1 Wash the fish several times in cold running water and dry it inside and out. Season the fish on the inside with salt and pepper.

2 Put the onion, celery, carrot, parsley and bay leaf in a fish kettle with the wine and vinegar. Bring to the boil. Lay the seasoned fish in the fish kettle and return it to the boil, covered.

3 Remove from the heat and leave to stand for about 15 minutes, or until the fish is cooked through: the fish is perfectly cooked when the eyes become opaque.

4 Remove the fish from the fish kettle and fillet it carefully. Serve the fillets drizzled with olive oil and lemon juice, garnished with chopped parsley and with lemon wedges on the side.

SERVES 4

1 sea bass, about 1.2kg/2½lb, scaled and cleaned
1 onion
1 celery stick
1 carrot
1 fresh parsley sprig
1 bay leaf
250ml/8fl oz/1 cup Trebbiano wine
30ml/2 tbsp white wine vinegar
sea salt and ground black pepper
olive oil, lemon juice, lemon wedges and chopped parsley, to serve

PER PORTION Energy 357kcal/1500kJ; Protein 58g; Carbohydrate 3g, of which sugars 3g; Fat 8g, of which saturates 1g; Cholesterol 240mg; Calcium 408mg; Fibre 0.6g; Sodium 216mg.

SERVES 4

juice of 1 lemon
4 monkfish fillets, about 200g/7oz each
about 12 sage leaves, roughly chopped
75ml/5 tbsp sunflower oil
8 slices prosciutto crudo (preferably prosciutto di Parma)
sea salt and ground black pepper
lemon wedges, to serve

MONKFISH WRAPPED IN PARMA HAM

CODA DI ROSPO VESTITA AL PROSCIUTTO DI PARMA

This is a recipe from the coast of Emilia-Romagna, which combines the sweet meatiness of locally caught monkfish with the salty-yet-sweet delight of Parma ham, or prosciutto di Parma. This unmistakable cured ham, which is used to envelop the fish, give it extra flavour and keep it perfectly moist, is one of the region's most famous products and it is exported throughout the world. If you like, you can use another type of prosciutto crudo instead.

1 Sprinkle lemon juice over the fish and season. Put on a plate and cover with clear film (plastic wrap). Leave in the refrigerator for 1 hour. Preheat the oven to 180°C/350°F/Gas 4.

2 Put the chopped sage in an ovenproof dish that is large enough to take the fish in a single layer. Drizzle over half the oil.

3 Wrap each fillet in two slices of prosciutto crudo, then lay the fillets in the ovenproof dish with the sage and the oil.

4 Drizzle the remaining oil over the wrapped fish. Bake in the preheated oven for 30 minutes, or until cooked through, then serve with lemon wedges.

PER PORTION Energy 390kcal/1630kJ; Protein 42g; Carbohydrate 0g, of which sugars 0g; Fat 25g, of which saturates 4g; Cholesterol 28mg; Calcium 16mg; Fibre 0g; Sodium 836mg.

SERVES 4

500g/1¼lb very fresh whitebait
30ml/2 tbsp chopped fresh flat leaf parsley
juice of 2 lemons
90ml/6 tbsp extra virgin olive oil
sea salt
lemon wedges, to serve

WHITEBAIT WITH LEMON
BIANCHETTI AL LIMONE

This Ligurian recipe for lemon-marinated whitebait is simplicity itself. The fish effectively 'cooks' in the citric acid of the lemon juice; there is no heat involved. Therefore, it is important to use fish that is absolutely fresh for this recipe.

1 Wash the fish thoroughly, then dry on kitchen paper. Arrange the whitebait on a large platter.

2 Sprinkle over the parsley and salt. Drizzle over the lemon juice and olive oil. Leave to marinate for 2 hours, then serve with lemon wedges.

PER PORTION Energy 418kcal/1734kJ; Protein 23g; Carbohydrate 0g, of which sugars 0g; Fat 36g, of which saturates 6g; Cholesterol 116mg; Calcium 122mg; Fibre 0g; Sodium 250mg.

STUFFED BABY SQUID

SEPPIOLINE RIPIENE

For this Ligurian dish, you need tender little squid that will hold their shape and look pretty once baked. Serve them on a bed of fresh salad leaves, such as peppery rocket (arugula), with lemon wedges for a lovely light meal.

SERVES 4

1.2kg/2½lb baby squid, cleaned and tubes left whole
4 salted anchovies, boned
115g/4oz/2 cups white breadcrumbs
2 garlic cloves, chopped
30ml/2 tbsp chopped fresh flat leaf parsley
75ml/5 tbsp extra virgin olive oil, plus extra for greasing
sea salt
salad leaves and lemon wedges, to serve

1 Preheat the oven to 200°C/400°F/Gas 6. Grease an ovenproof dish with olive oil.

2 Rinse the squid repeatedly in running cold water until they are pure white and no sand or grit remains inside the tubes.

3 Wash the anchovies then chop finely. Mix the breadcrumbs, anchovies, garlic, parsley and salt together. Stir in one-third of the olive oil.

4 Fill the squid with the stuffing and seal the opening with a wooden cocktail stick (toothpick). You may not use all of the stuffing.

5 Arrange the stuffed squid in the ovenproof dish and sprinkle with any remaining filling. Drizzle over the remaining olive oil.

6 Bake for 20 minutes, until golden. Serve on a bed of salad leaves, with lemon wedges.

PER PORTION Energy 521kcal/2191kJ; Protein 50g; Carbohydrate 26g, of which sugars 1g; Fat 25g, of which saturates 4g; Cholesterol 677mg; Calcium 89mg; Fibre 0.8g; Sodium 667mg.

POULTRY, MEAT AND GAME

POLLAME, CARNE E CACCIA

Beef, veal and game really come into their own in Lombardy, Piedmont and the Aosta Valley, while Liguria has a selection of veal dishes to call its own, too. There is some lamb on the menu, but it is really chicken and veal that take centre stage in this part of Italy. Emilia-Romagna, on the other hand, places the most emphasis on cured pork, which is celebrated in different ways: from many varieties of salami to the enormous, pink mortadella and the world-famous prosciutto di Parma. Pigs have been reared in the region since at least 1000BC, and prosciutto has reigned supreme in the town of Parma for hundreds of years. Not to be forgotten in this vast range of expertly cured meats is the salama da sugo from Ferrara. This region also uses horsemeat to make a very traditional local dish called la picula, and the city of Piacenza boasts a stew made from donkey meat!

BRAISED BEEF, QUICK-FRIED VEAL AND BOLLITO MISTO

The age-old tradition of hunting, and the once plentiful variety of furred and feathered game means that the local menus of the Aosta Valley, Piedmont and Lombardy are liberally peppered with game dishes. Game is often cooked in the local wines: the famous white Arneis of Piedmont, for example, is used to prepare one of the region's delicious hare stews, and guinea fowl is cooked in the sensational Barolo wine for a truly indulgent dish. Chicken is also common on the local menus, with the historic dish of pollo alla Marengo being one of the most popular. It has an intriguing ingredients list and serves as a historic reminder of one of Napoleon's greatest battles.

These are also the regions where veal and beef are truly celebrated and are cooked with skill in a magnificent array of recipes, ranging from effortlessly simple dishes to elegant and elaborate main courses. The deliciously easy costoletta alla Milanese is the epitome of true Lombard veal simplicity, where a thick veal cutlet is coated in breadcrumbs before being fried in a sea of melted butter. Beef is often beaten very thinly and then rolled round a tasty filling, which has long been a clever way of making scraps of meat into a cheap meal.

The vast bollito misto, that ceremonious dish of boiled meats, such as beef, veal, tongue and cotechino, is common in Lombardy, Emilia-Romagna and Piedmont. Each region, however, rings the changes slightly, serving this monumental feast with their own specially created sauces, which can include mostarda di Cremona and piquant salsa verde.

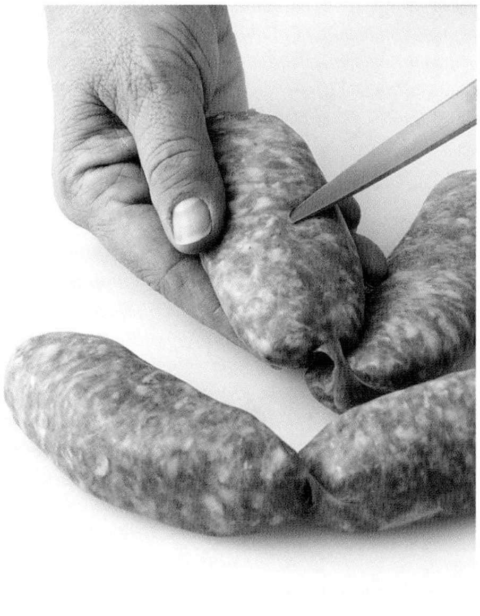
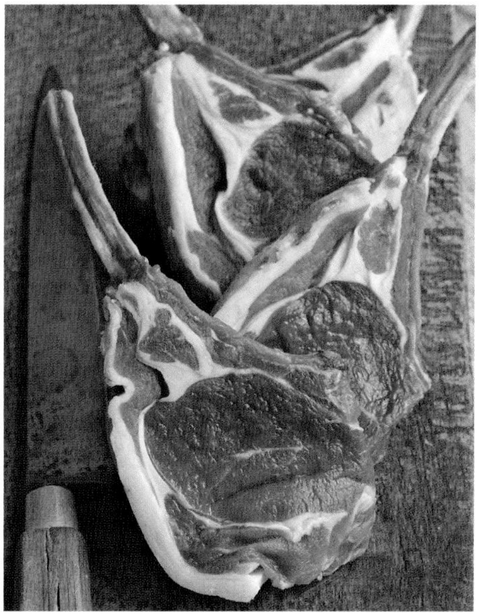

CHICKEN BREAST IN THE MODENESE STYLE
PETTO DI POLLO ALLA MODENESE

This is a dish from Modena, which uses local produce in the form of mortadella and Parmesan, finished off with rich and indulgent cream for good measure! You might like to add a little shaving of black or white truffles just before serving.

1 Trim the chicken breast fillets and lay them between sheets of clear film (plastic wrap). Bash them lightly with a rolling pin to a thickness of 2cm/¾in to form escalopes (scallops). Toss them lightly in the flour, then season with salt and pepper.

2 Melt the butter in a large frying pan, add the floured chicken and cook for 4–5 minutes on each side, until golden and cooked through. You will probably need to cook two at a time.

3 Lay a slice of mortadella over the top of each chicken breast (while still in the frying pan) and distribute the grated Parmesan cheese over the top of each.

4 Pour the cream around the chicken, cover the pan and cook for 5 minutes, or until the cheese has melted. Serve the chicken with the cream spooned over, topped with a little extra grated Parmesan, and accompanied by green beans.

SERVES 6

6 skinless chicken breast fillets
60ml/4 tbsp plain (all-purpose) flour
75g/3oz/6 tbsp unsalted butter
6 slices mortadella
65g/2½oz/¾ cup freshly grated Parmesan cheese, plus extra to serve
90ml/6 tbsp double (heavy) cream
sea salt and ground black pepper
green beans, to serve

PER PORTION Energy 445kcal/1867kJ; Protein 43g; Carbohydrate 8g, of which sugars 1g; Fat 27g, of which saturates 16g; Cholesterol 173mg; Calcium 145mg; Fibre 0.3g; Sodium 276mg.

SERVES 4

1.2kg/2½lb chicken, jointed
60ml/4 tbsp plain (all-purpose) flour
175ml/6fl oz/¾ cup, plus 60ml/4 tbsp, olive oil, plus extra if needed
400g/14oz canned tomatoes, seeded and chopped
5 basil leaves, tied together with white cotton
175ml/6fl oz/¾ cup dry white wine
1 garlic clove, crushed
200g/7oz/3 cups mushrooms, thickly sliced
4 slices white bread, such as ciabatta
4 eggs
30ml/2 tbsp finely chopped parsley, plus extra to garnish
juice of 1 lemon, strained
sea salt and ground black pepper

PER PORTION Energy 974kcal/4056kJ; Protein 59g; Carbohydrate 33g, of which sugars 5g; Fat 65g, of which saturates 12g; Cholesterol 415mg; Calcium 158mg; Fibre 2.6g; Sodium 439mg.

CHICKEN MARENGO
POLLO ALLA MARENGO

This dish was apparently served to Napoleon and his officers at the end of the Battle of Marengo, using only what remained on the cook's cart. This explains, one can only presume, the slightly weird combination of ingredients. They taste good, nevertheless. This dish is often served with prawns (shrimp) on top of each egg. If you want to add them, cook the unpeeled prawns in white wine with a good pinch of salt for about 5 minutes until cooked through.

1 Wash the chicken joints and pat them dry with kitchen paper. Put the flour on a plate or in a plastic bag and use to dust the chicken all over. Season the chicken with salt and pepper.

2 Heat the 175ml/6fl oz/¾ cup of oil in a wide pan, add the chicken and fry for 15 minutes, turning occasionally, until browned all over.

3 Add the tomatoes, basil and wine to the chicken. Then add the crushed garlic and a little salt. Stir and cover, then cook for a further 15 minutes.

4 Add the mushrooms, cover again and cook for 10 minutes more.

5 Heat the 60ml/4 tbsp oil in a separate frying pan, add the bread and fry until crisp and golden. Remove and set aside. Fry the eggs in the same frying pan; you may need a little more oil.

6 Sprinkle the parsley over the chicken, pour over the lemon juice and stir.

7 Using a slotted spoon, remove the chicken from the pan and arrange on a platter. Discard the basil. Surround with the sauce and mushrooms, then arrange the fried bread around the edge. Put an egg on each slice of bread. Serve immediately, sprinkled with extra chopped parsley.

SERVES 4

- 1 whole chicken, about 1.6kg/3½lb, jointed
- 2 large ripe tomatoes
- 115g/4oz streaky (fatty) bacon, lard or white cooking fat, chopped
- 1 large onion, finely chopped
- 1 small bunch celery leaves, chopped
- 1 small sprig each of fresh rosemary, sage and parsley, leaves chopped
- 50g/2oz juniper berries, lightly crushed
- 250ml/8fl oz/1 cup dry red wine
- 250ml/8fl oz/1 cup chicken stock
- salt and ground black pepper
- chopped fresh parsley, to garnish
- mashed potatoes or soft polenta, to serve

CHICKEN WITH JUNIPER
POLLO AL GINEPRO

This is a chicken casserole from the Aosta Valley with lots of flavoursome ingredients, including red wine and scented herbs, as well as lightly crushed juniper berries, which have a warming quality. Serve with a mound of soft polenta or mashed potatoes.

1 Wash the chicken joints and dry thoroughly on kitchen paper. Plunge the tomatoes into boiling water for 30 seconds, then refresh in cold water. Peel away the skins, remove the seeds and chop the flesh. Discard the skin and seeds, and set the chopped flesh aside.

2 Heat the bacon or fat in a large frying pan, add the onion, celery leaves, herbs and juniper berries and cook over a medium heat for 5 minutes or until the onion is soft.

3 Add the chicken joints and brown them thoroughly on all sides. Pour the wine over the chicken and cook for 3–4 minutes to allow the alcohol to burn off. Add the tomatoes and the stock, then stir thoroughly.

4 Season with salt and pepper, then cover and simmer for 90 minutes, basting occasionally with the hot stock, until the chicken is cooked through and tender. Serve on mashed potatoes or polenta, sprinkled with chopped parsley.

PER PORTION Energy 365kcal/1525kJ; Protein 38g; Carbohydrate 7g, of which sugars 6g; Fat 16g, of which saturates 5g; Cholesterol 147mg; Calcium 53mg; Fibre 1.7g; Sodium 638mg.

GUINEA FOWL WITH BAROLO
FARAONA AL BAROLO

For people who are not sure about game, guinea fowl is the perfect bird as it has only a slight gamey flavour. If you cannot find any, the same dish works well with a small, free-range chicken. For a larger chicken, just increase the ingredients accordingly.

SERVES 4

1 guinea fowl, about 1kg/2¼lb
10g/¼oz/2 tbsp dried porcini mushrooms
50g/2oz pork fat, chopped
50g/2oz/¼ cup unsalted butter
200g/7oz shallots or baby (pearl) onions, chopped
20g/¾oz/3 tbsp plain (all-purpose) flour
1 litre/1¾ pints/4 cups Barolo wine
60ml/4 tbsp grappa
pinch of grated nutmeg
1 luganega sausage, peeled and chopped
sea salt and ground black pepper
chopped fresh parsley, to garnish
mashed potatoes, to serve

1 Wipe the guinea fowl and joint it. Set aside. Put the porcini mushrooms in 200ml/7fl oz/ scant 1 cup warm water to soak.

2 Put the pork fat and half the butter in a large frying pan and cook the onions for 5 minutes, until soft.

3 Add the guinea fowl and cook briefly on all sides, then sprinkle with flour and turn the pieces several times until the flour is absorbed into the fat. Pour over the wine and grappa, and stir. Add the nutmeg and seasoning.

4 Boil for 2 minutes, then reduce the heat and simmer for 1 hour, or until tender. Remove the joints from the pan, set aside and keep warm.

5 Increase the heat under the sauce and reduce it by one-third. Add the drained porcini and the chopped sausage. Cook together for 15 minutes, or until the sauce has thickened and the sausage is cooked through.

6 Serve the guinea fowl on mashed potatoes, with the sauce poured over, garnished with chopped parsley.

PER PORTION Energy 685kcal/2854kJ; Protein 40g; Carbohydrate 9g, of which sugars 4g; Fat 36g, of which saturates 16g; Cholesterol 119mg; Calcium 72mg; Fibre 0.9g; Sodium 210mg.

BOLOGNESE LAMB CUTLETS
COSTOLETTE D'AGNELLO ALLA BOLOGNESE

In this recipe, lamb cutlets are coated in breadcrumbs and fried until crisp, then topped with mozzarella and prosciutto before a few moments in the oven to melt the cheese to a satisfying ooze. You could use tiny cutlets for a party dish to eat with the fingers.

1 Preheat the oven to 220°C/425°F/Gas 7. Trim the cutlets carefully and flatten them as much as possible with a meat mallet.

2 Put the flour on a plate and lightly flour the cutlets, then dip them in the egg, and finally in the breadcrumbs.

3 Heat the oil in a frying pan until sizzling, and then fry the lamb cutlets on each side until golden brown and crisp.

4 Remove from the pan, and drain thoroughly on kitchen paper. Season to taste.

5 Arrange the cutlets on a baking tray, lay a slice of prosciutto and a slice of mozzarella cheese on each cutlet and bake in the oven for 5 minutes, or until the cheese begins to run.

6 Serve the lamb immediately, with some roasted vegetables.

SERVES 6

12 lamb cutlets (US rib chops)
20g/¾oz/3 tbsp plain (all-purpose) flour
2 eggs, beaten
75ml/5 tbsp dried white breadcrumbs (see Cook's Tip)
90ml/6 tbsp olive oil
115g/4oz prosciutto crudo, sliced thinly (preferably prosciutto di Parma)
150g/5oz mozzarella cheese, cut into 12 slices
sea salt and ground black pepper
roasted vegetables, to serve

COOK'S TIP

If possible, try to use Italian breadcrumbs, pangrattato, which are really fine and made with good-quality bread. If you cannot get hold of these, it is best to make your own in a food processor by grinding stale bread to very fine crumbs.

PER PORTION Energy 588kcal/2453kJ; Protein 43g; Carbohydrate 17g, of which sugars 0g; Fat 39g, of which saturates 14g; Cholesterol 192mg; Calcium 156mg; Fibre 0.6g; Sodium 690mg.

SERVES 4

115g/4oz of stale white bread, soaked in milk to cover, until soft
200g/7oz Italian sausage meat (bulk sausage)
2 egg yolks
30ml/2 tbsp freshly grated Parmesan cheese
1kg/2¼lb of fillet steak (beef tenderloin)
300g/11oz fruit mustard (preferably mostarda di Cremona)
25g/1oz/2 tbsp unsalted butter
60ml/4 tbsp dry white wine
sea salt and ground black pepper

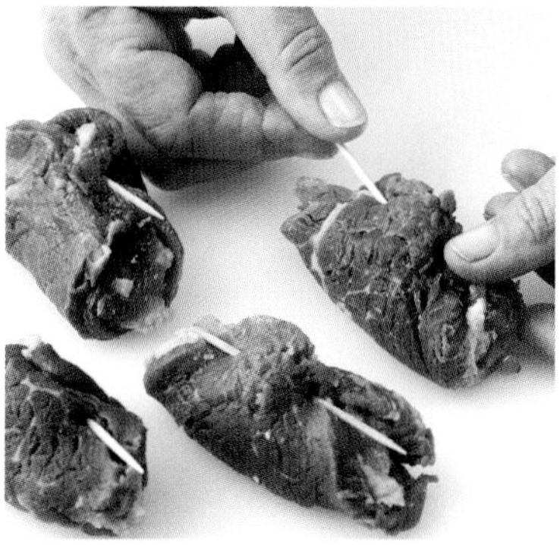

STEAK ROLLS WITH FRUIT MUSTARD
INVOLTINI ALLA MOSTARDA DI CREMONA

What makes this dish special is the use of mostarda di Cremona, the closest Italian cuisine comes to a kind of chutney. It is made with candied fruits in a heavy mustard syrup and is usually served with cheese or meat dishes such as Bollito Misto.

1 Squeeze the bread dry. In a bowl, mix the sausage meat with the bread, egg yolks, Parmesan cheese, and salt and pepper to create a smooth mixture.

2 Slice the fillet steak into eight even portions. Beat the steaks with a meat mallet or rolling pin until 2cm/¾in thick.

3 Spread sausage mixture over the top of each steak. Take 40ml/8 tsp of the fruit mustard and cut it up into small pieces. Add 5ml/1 tsp fruit mustard to each steak. Roll up the steaks and secure with a cocktail stick (toothpick) or string.

4 Melt the butter in a large frying pan, add the steak rolls and cook for 8–10 minutes, turning often, until cooked evenly. Keep warm.

5 Keep the pan over a low heat, add the wine and 30ml/2 tbsp water, then raise the heat and boil quickly together, scraping the sides and base of the pan to incorporate any scraps.

6 Return the steak rolls to the pan and heat through for 3–4 minutes. Add water if needed.

7 Serve immediately, with the sauce poured over and with the remaining fruit mustard.

PER PORTION Energy 347kcal/825kJ; Protein 74g; Carbohydrate 4g, of which sugars 2g; Fat 49g, of which saturates 22g; Cholesterol 302mg; Calcium 158mg; Fibre 0.9g; Sodium 1018mg.

BRAISED BEEF IN BAROLO
BRASATO AL BAROLO

This classic meat dish from Piedmont is often served with steaming hot slabs of polenta. It is very satisfying and filling, and it allows all the flavour of the wine to shine through. It is not true that cooking wine can be of a lesser quality than the wine you choose to drink, especially when using a really good, carefully selected joint of beef. Barolo is famously expensive, but deservedly so. With this in mind, this dish could be reserved to impress your guests at a dinner party.

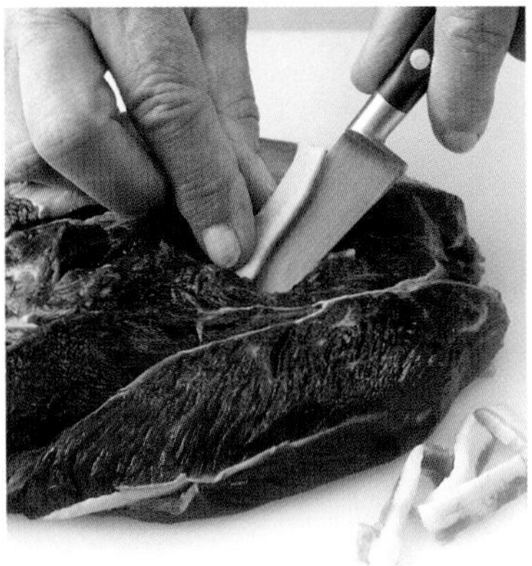

1 Pierce the joint all over with a sharp knife or thick skewer and insert the strips of pork fat deep into the meat.

2 Mix the chopped parsley, sage, rosemary and garlic together. Add plenty of salt and pepper and then stir in the nutmeg, mixed spice and half the flour.

3 Heat the oil and butter together in a large, heavy flameproof casserole until the butter is melted and lightly foaming, then add the onion. Let the onion sizzle gently for a 3–4 minutes, stirring.

4 Meanwhile, roll the joint in the herb mixture. Lay it gently on top of the frying onion.

5 Add the carrot, celery, bay leaves and parsley sprigs. Seal the meat all over, turning it several times until browned, then remove it from the casserole.

6 Carefully drain off any excess fat from the casserole, then add the remaining flour and stir it into the juices, onions, carrots, celery and herbs that remain in the casserole to make a roux.

7 Pour in 350ml/12fl oz/1½ cups of red wine and stir together thoroughly. Cook for about 2 minutes to allow the alcohol to evaporate, then return the meat to the casserole. Turn it over several times, then add the rest of the wine and cover the casserole tightly with a lid.

8 Lower the heat to the lowest setting and simmer as gently as possible for about 4 hours, turning the joint occasionally, until the meat is completely tender.

9 Remove the meat from the casserole and set aside. Remove and set aside a few chunks of carrot and celery, then push the sauce through a food mill or wide-meshed sieve (strainer). Season to taste, then put the vegetable chunks back into the sauce.

10 Slice the meat thickly, then serve it on top of slices of warm polenta or mounds of mashed potatoes, with the sauce poured over.

SERVES 6

2.5kg/5½lb beef stewing joint, such as brisket or shin (shank)
50g/2oz pork fat, cut into thin strips
30ml/2 tbsp chopped fresh parsley
5ml/1 tsp chopped fresh sage
7.5ml/1½ tsp chopped fresh rosemary
2 garlic cloves, finely chopped
pinch of grated nutmeg
pinch of mixed (apple pie) spice
30g/1¼oz/5 tbsp plain (all-purpose) flour
75ml/5 tbsp olive oil
15g/½oz/1 tbsp unsalted butter
1 onion, chopped
1 carrot, sliced
1 celery stick, sliced
2 bay leaves
3–4 small fresh parsley sprigs
750ml/1¼ pints/3 cups Barolo wine
sea salt and ground black pepper
polenta slices or mashed potatoes, to serve

PER PORTION Energy 906kcal/3777kJ; Protein 89g; Carbohydrate 7g, of which sugars 3g; Fat 48g, of which saturates 19g; Cholesterol 268mg; Calcium 47mg; Fibre 1g; Sodium 200mg.

SERVES 4

8 thinly sliced beef minute steaks or veal escalopes (US veal scallops)
75ml/5 tbsp extra virgin olive oil
1 celery stick, chopped
1 carrot, chopped
1 small onion, chopped
175ml/6fl oz/¾ cup dry white wine
200g/7oz fresh or frozen peas
300ml/½ pint/1¼ cups vegetable stock

FOR THE FILLING

200g/7oz chard, steamed, drained and finely chopped
200g/7oz spinach, steamed, drained and finely chopped
50g/2oz/⅔ cup freshly grated Parmesan cheese
20g/¾oz/6 tbsp dried porcini mushrooms, soaked in warm water for 30 minutes, drained and chopped
10g/¼oz/1 tbsp toasted pine nuts
2 eggs, beaten
30ml/2 tbsp chopped fresh flat leaf parsley
a fresh marjoram sprig, leaves removed and chopped
1 garlic clove, chopped
sea salt

TOMASELLE
LE TOMAXÆLLE

This is a Ligurian interpretation of an ancient recipe, which could date back as far as the 15th century. It would have been a clever way of making scraps of cheap meat go further, by putting a filling inside, then cooking it in a sauce to make it tender.

1 Beat the meat with a meat mallet or rolling pin until almost transparent and each slice is about the same size as the palm of your hand.

2 Mix together all the ingredients for the filling and season with salt. Divide between the meat slices, then roll each slice up, tucking in the ends. Tie securely with cook's string.

3 Pour the olive oil into a large frying pan and add the celery, carrot and onion. Fry gently for 5–10 minutes until just softened and brown.

4 Add the meat rolls and cook, turning them over frequently, until they are browned on all sides.

5 Pour in the wine, then add the peas and continue to cook gently for 1 hour, or until the meat rolls are cooked through, gradually adding vegetable stock as necessary to prevent the rolls from drying out.

6 Remove the string from the meat rolls and serve immediately, with the peas and sauce.

PER PORTION Energy 502kcal/2096kJ; Protein 46g; Carbohydrate 10g, of which sugars 5g; Fat 28g, of which saturates 6g; Cholesterol 90mg; Calcium 277mg; Fibre 5.2g; Sodium 506mg.

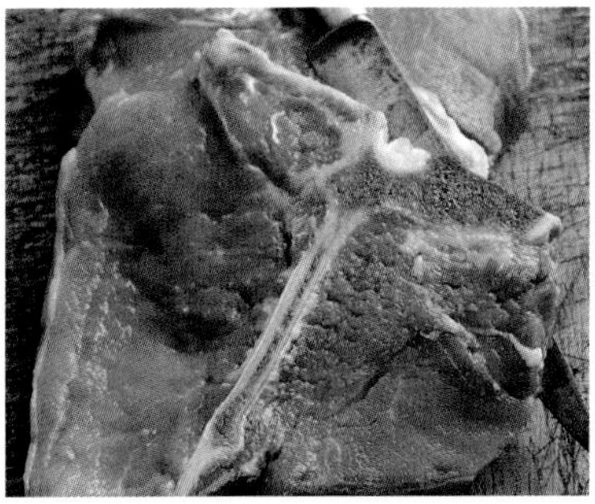

VEAL CHOP MILANESE STYLE
COSTOLETTA ALLA MILANESE

This is an incredibly rich dish, even though it contains only a few ingredients, as a generous amount of butter is used to cook the chops. It shows off the flavour of the meat perfectly and needs just some steamed vegetables and lemon wedges to serve.

SERVES 4

8 veal chops
600ml/1 pint/2½ cups milk
2 eggs, beaten
75g/3oz dried white breadcrumbs
115g/4oz/½ cup unsalted butter
sea salt and ground black pepper
steamed vegetables and lemon wedges, to serve

1 Beat the veal chops with a meat mallet or rolling pin to about 2cm/¾in thickness. Soak them in the milk for 30 minutes.

2 Remove the veal chops from the milk and dip them into the beaten egg and then into the breadcrumbs, pressing the crumbs firmly and evenly on to the meat with the palm of your hand.

3 Melt the butter in a large frying pan over a medium heat, add the breaded chops and fry for 3 minutes on each side; turn them only once. The crust should be golden brown and the meat pink. You may need to fry the veal in batches.

4 Season to taste, then serve, with vegetables and lemon wedges for squeezing over.

COOK'S TIP

A lighter version, known as cotolette, uses veal escalopes (US veal scallops) instead. Fry the escalopes for 4 minutes on each side until crisp and golden. You can also use turkey or chicken, if you like.

PER PORTION Energy 527kcal/2221kJ; Protein 40g; Carbohydrate 22g, of which sugars 8g; Fat 32g, of which saturates 19g; Cholesterol 256mg; Calcium 232mg; Fibre 0.4g; Sodium 327mg.

VEAL WITH MARSALA
SCALOPPINE AL MARSALA

The scaloppina is an integral part of every Italian kitchen. There are many versions: with wine, with herbs, with orange or lemon juice and grated rind, with vin Santo, and lots of others. Here is the classic Marsala version from Piedmont.

1 Beat the meat carefully with a meat mallet or rolling pin until very thin. Put the flour on a plate and, just before you are ready to fry it, lightly coat the veal in the flour.

2 Heat the butter in a large frying pan and quickly fry the meat for 2 minutes on each side. Season with salt and pepper. Remove the meat from the pan and keep warm.

3 Pour the Marsala into the hot pan. Cook for 2 minutes over a high heat to allow the alcohol to evaporate, scraping the base of the pan to amalgamate the juices from the meat and the butter. Lower the heat a little, then cook, stirring to reduce the sauce slightly.

4 Serve the veal on top of mashed potatoes, with the sauce poured over.

SERVES 4

8 veal escalopes (US veal scallops), trimmed
15–20g/$^{1}/_{2}$–$^{3}/_{4}$oz/2–3 tbsp plain (all-purpose) flour
50g/2oz/$^{1}/_{4}$ cup unsalted butter
175ml/6fl oz/$^{3}/_{4}$ cup Marsala
sea salt and ground black pepper
mashed potatoes, to serve

PER PORTION Energy 299kcal/1260kJ; Protein 35g; Carbohydrate 4g, of which sugars 2g; Fat 13g, of which saturates 8g; Cholesterol 107mg; Calcium 18mg; Fibre 0.2g; Sodium 93mg.

SERVES 6

1.5kg/3¼lb ossobucco or thick cut veal shanks
4 celery sticks, finely chopped
1 large onion, finely chopped
2 carrots, finely chopped
3 garlic cloves, finely chopped
60ml/4 tbsp olive oil
750ml/1¼ pints/3 cups dry white wine
250ml/8fl oz/1 cup passata (bottled strained tomatoes)
30ml/2 tbsp tomato purée (paste), diluted in 45ml/3 tbsp warm water
sea salt and ground black pepper
plain risotto and gremolata (see Cook's Tip), to serve

COOK'S TIP

To make gremolata mix finely chopped fresh flat leaf parsley with grated lemon rind, salt and ground black pepper.

PER PORTION Energy 347kcal/1448kJ; Protein 28g; Carbohydrate 9g, of which sugars 7g; Fat 14g, of which saturates 3g; Cholesterol 105mg; Calcium 54mg; Fibre 2g; Sodium 195mg.

STEWED OSSOBUCCO
OSSOBUCO IN UMIDO

The dish from Lombardy is traditionally served on a plain white or a saffron risotto, or on mashed potato, with gremolata, a piquant mixture of chopped flat leaf parsley and grated lemon rind, sprinkled on top.

1 Wipe the veal to make sure there are no shards of bone. Put the oil, all the vegetables, and the garlic into a heavy frying pan that is large enough to take all the meat as well. Fry for 10 minutes, or until softened.

2 Remove the vegetables and set aside. Add the meat to the pan and brown carefully on both sides.

3 Add half the wine and boil quickly over a high heat for 1 minute to evaporate the alcohol, then lower the heat and add the passata and the tomato purée. Season and cover, then simmer for 2 hours, stirring fairly frequently and adding the remaining wine, a little at a time to keep it moist, until very tender.

4 Serve on plain risotto, topped with gremolata.

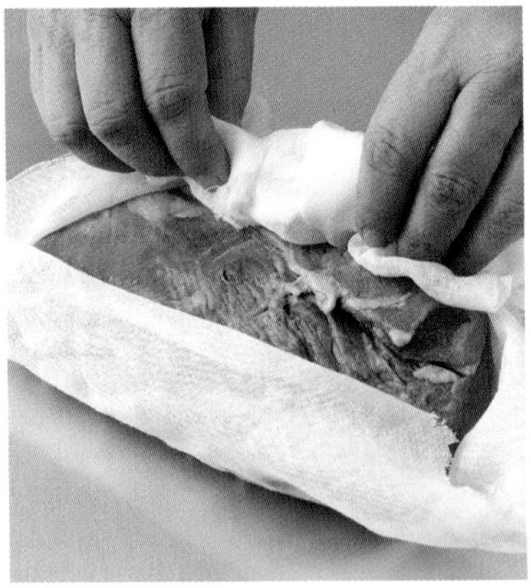

COLD VEAL WITH TUNA MAYONNAISE
VITELLO TONNATO

This is a real summer favourite all over Lombardy and other areas of north-west Italy where you can always find this dish ready-made at good delicatessens when the weather gets hot. Although the combination of boiled meat and tuna mayonnaise might seem a little odd, when put together in this way it makes a very special dish. It needs only a green salad and some pickles to make a lovely meal. Don't serve the dish too cold or it will lose its delicate flavour. Start preparations the day before.

1 Lay the joint of veal in a deep bowl. First, make the marinade. Set aside 175ml/6fl oz/¾ cup of the white wine and pour the rest of the wine into a bowl. Add all the other marinade ingredients to the wine and mix together.

2 Pour the marinade over the meat and leave to stand in the refrigerator overnight.

3 The next day, drain the meat from the marinade, and wrap it in muslin (cheesecloth). Tie it up tightly using cook's string, then lay it in a deep pan.

4 Pour the marinade and the stock over the meat and boil it slowly for 1½ hours, or until the veal is completely cooked through. Leave the meat to cool in the marinade.

5 Take the meat out of the cold marinade and unwrap the muslin. Slice the meat thinly and arrange on a large platter.

6 To make the sauce, mix the mayonnaise with the canned tuna, capers, and the reserved white wine, and season with salt and pepper.

7 Drizzle the sauce over the sliced meat. Serve immediately with green salad, capers, gherkins and lemon wedges on the side, and garnish with chopped parsley. Alternatively, chill until required.

SERVES 6

900g/2lb veal fillet joint
600ml/1 pint/2½ cups veal or chicken stock
green salad, capers, gherkins and lemon wedges, to serve
chopped parsley, to garnish

FOR THE MARINADE

750ml/1¼ pints/3 cups dry white wine
1 onion, sliced
1 carrot, sliced
4 cloves
3 bay leaves, chopped
salt and ground black pepper

FOR THE SAUCE

300g/11oz thick mayonnaise, (see Cook's Tip)
185g/6½oz canned tuna in olive oil, drained and finely flaked
200g/7oz capers preserved in salt or vinegar, rinsed, dried and finely chopped
sea salt and ground black pepper

COOK'S TIP

To make mayonnaise without hours of patient whisking, put 1 egg into the bowl of the food processor and whiz until pale yellow. Mix together 150ml/¼ pint/⅔ cup each of sunflower and extra virgin olive oil, then gradually add to the egg in a very thin, slow, steady stream, keeping the motor running. The oil and egg will emulsify into a thick, smooth and pale sauce. Add the juice of ½ lemon, or to taste, and season.

PER PORTION Energy 669kcal/2779kJ; Protein 41g; Carbohydrate 6g, of which sugars 4g; Fat 45g, of which saturates 8g; Cholesterol 179mg; Calcium 47mg; Fibre 0.7g; Sodium 998mg.

BOLLITO MISTO
BOLLITO MISTO

This is one of Italy's great celebratory dishes, and a favourite to be served on special occasions. It is actually a simple combination of all kinds of meat, boiled together with vegetables. Of course, the secret to a delicious combination starts with high-quality ingredients, so that their flavours will stand out even after hours of simmering. It is important to serve the dish with various sauces, such as Salsa Verde and the ubiquitous accompaniment for bollito misto: mostarda di Cremona, which consists of glacé (candied) fruits preserved in a heavy mustard syrup. The idea of serving sauces that have a sweet-and-sour or piquant taste with the meats is to help to enliven the various distinctive flavours.

SERVES 8

600g/1lb 6oz cotechino
1 boiling fowl
8 peppercorns
2 large onions
8 cloves
2 large carrots
3 celery sticks
2 bay leaves
675g/1½lb veal breast
675g/1½lb beef shin (shank) or skirt (flank)
675g/1½lb veal silverside (pot roast)
1 ready-to-cook tongue (see Cook's Tip)
sea salt
Salsa Verde and mustards, including mostarda di Cremona, to serve

1 Pierce the cotechino all over with the point of a knife and put into a large pan. Cover with cold water and leave to soak for 1 hour.

2 Drain and cover with fresh water, then bring to the boil and simmer gently for 3 hours.

3 Put the boiling fowl into a second large pan and cover with cold water. Add 4 peppercorns, 1 onion stuck with 4 cloves, 1 carrot, 1 stick of celery, 1 bay leaf and a good pinch of salt. Bring to the boil and simmer gently for 3 hours.

4 Put the veal breast, beef shin or skirt and the veal silverside it into a third large pan with the remaining peppercorns, onion stuck with cloves, carrot, celery sticks, bay leaf and a good pinch of salt. Cover with cold water and bring to the boil. Reduce the heat and simmer gently for 3 hours.

5 After 1 hour of cooking, put the tongue in a fourth pan with cold water to cover, and bring to the boil. Simmer for 2 hours.

6 When all the meat is cooked, transfer it all to a warmed casserole, discarding the studded onions, bay leaves and all the excess liquid.

7 Serve from the casserole, removing the various elements and carving them at the table on a large board. Each serving should contain a little of each type of meat and a slice each of carrot and celery for colour. Serve it piping hot, with Salsa Verde and a selection of mustards.

COOK'S TIP

You will need to ask a butcher for ready-to-cook tongue as it is not usually available in supermarkets.

PER PORTION Energy 740kcal/3048kJ; Protein 76g; Carbohydrate 11g, of which sugars 6g; Fat 44g, of which saturates 12g; Cholesterol 332mg; Calcium 166mg; Fibre 1.4g; Sodium 1268mg.

EGGS, VEGETABLES AND CHEESE

UOVA, VERDURE E FORMAGGIO

The best of local vegetables are celebrated by cooks in north-west Italy as they come into season. Local cooks treat vegetables with the utmost respect, and many vegetable dishes can be turned into a light meal in themselves. These regions may not celebrate the tomato with quite the same fervour as their southern cousins, but they know how to cook a whole variety of other vegetables, including courgettes (zucchini), fennel and artichokes, with a light touch and elegance that does not mask the freshness of the ingredients. Liguria is famous for its vegetable pies and tarts, all of which are liberally flavoured with the variety of fresh herbs which the local cooks use so expertly. Basil is used to make the ubiquitous Pesto, the culinary symbol of Liguria. Eggs and local cheeses including Parmesan, Fontina and Taleggio are used to make a variety of rich dishes.

FONTINA, PARMESAN AND SALSA VERDE

Eggs are an inexpensive and nutritious ingredient that are used all over Italy, with the north-western area being no exception. Nourishing frittatas are made with a medley of vegetables and a little local cheese, and they are sustaining enough to be served as a meal on their own. Eggs are also combined with famous cheeses from these regions to create other rich dishes. Piedmontese Fonduta is similar to a Swiss fondue, made with delicious Fontina cheese from the Aosta Valley. Another hearty cheesy treat is the Piedmontese Baked Egg and Cheese Custard, which is made with Parmesan. Both of these dishes are typically served with Italian breadsticks called grissini.

Many vegetables are cooked in a way known as 'alla Parmigiana', literally meaning 'from the city of Parma', but it usually means the vegetables are simply cooked by steaming or boiling, coated in plenty of butter and copious amounts of freshly grated Parmesan, then lightly grilled before serving. This delightfully simple way of serving vegetables is perfect to transform them into a light lunch or supper dish, with perhaps some good bread, a salad and some local wine. This method is often used to prepare fennel and asparagus, as well as many other vegetables that grow in the rich and fertile soil of the largely flat Emilia-Romagna.

Worth a special mention is the famous Salsa Verde, which originated in Piedmont and is now prepared all over the world. It is made with an array of flavoursome ingredients, including anchovies, capers, garlic and parsley, and is an excellent accompaniment to poached fish. It is also served with the classic dish Bollito Misto.

POTATO AND LEEK FRITTATA WITH TALEGGIO
FRITTATA AL TALEGGIO CON PORRI E PATATE

This frittata is substantial enough to serve as a one-pot meal on a hot summer day and is lovely at room temperature with a glass of refreshing white wine and some crisp green salad. Taleggio is a nutty, semi-soft cow's milk cheese that has been produced in Lombardy since the Middle Ages. It has a subtle truffle aroma, especially close to its rind, which imparts a unique taste to this dish. It might be difficult to find in supermarkets, but you should be able to find it in good Italian delicatessens.

1 Heat half the olive oil in a 30cm/12in non-stick frying pan over a medium heat. Add the leeks, potato, onion and beans. Season with salt and pepper. Cover with a tight-fitting lid and cook, stirring frequently, for 10 minutes.

2 Lower the heat to medium-low and cook, uncovered, for 10 minutes more, or until the potato is tender and the mixture is fairly dry.

3 Meanwhile, put the eggs into a large mixing bowl, add the basil and a pinch of salt and pepper, and beat to mix well.

4 Stir the hot potato and vegetable mixture into the bowl with the eggs, stirring constantly to avoid scrambling the eggs.

5 Pour the remaining olive oil into the frying pan and heat over a medium-high heat for 1 minute.

6 Pour in the egg and vegetable mixture, allow to cook for 1 minute, then sprinkle the cubes of Taleggio cheese over the top.

7 Shake the pan to flatten and even out the mixture, pulling the liquid egg into the centre as you work. Cook for about 8 minutes until the underside is browned and firm.

8 Turn the frittata over by covering the frying pan with a large lid or plate and overturning the frying pan on to it. Put the frying pan back down on to the heat and carefully slide the frittata, uncooked side down, back into the hot pan.

9 Cook again for about 5 minutes, until golden brown and firm on the underside. Slide the frittata out on to a clean, flat plate and serve either hot or cold, sliced into chunky wedges, accompanied by a green salad.

SERVES 6

30ml/2 tbsp extra virgin olive oil
3 leeks, cut in half lengthways, and thinly sliced
1 large potato, peeled, quartered and thinly sliced
1 onion, thinly sliced
200g/7oz green beans, trimmed and cut into 5mm/¼in lengths
6 eggs
8 fresh basil leaves, torn
200g/7oz Taleggio, rind removed and the cheese roughly cut into 1cm/½in cubes
sea salt and ground black pepper
green salad, to serve

PER PORTION Energy 325kcal/1353kJ; Protein 22g; Carbohydrate 10g, of which sugars 4g; Fat 22g, of which saturates 9g; Cholesterol 263mg; Calcium 408mg; Fibre 2.5g; Sodium 341mg.

SERVES 4

450g/1lb Fontina cheese, cubed
15ml/1 tbsp plain (all-purpose) flour or polenta flour
200ml/7fl oz/scant 1 cup cold milk
4 egg yolks
115g/4oz/½ cup butter
toasted bread, to serve

PIEDMONTESE FONDUTA

FONDUTA ALLA PIEMONTESE

The Italian version of a Swiss cheese fondue, fonduta, is served as a dip or over pasta, polenta or risotto. It is incredibly rich, so only a small amount is needed to make you feel really full! It also tastes good with toasted or fried bread or grissini (breadsticks).

1 In a deep stainless-steel pan, mix the cheese and the flour or polenta together thoroughly. Cover with the milk and leave to soften for 30 minutes. Drain the cheese.

2 Put the egg yolks and butter into the top half of a double boiler, or in a heatproof bowl over simmering water.

3 Add the cheese, and stir constantly until the cheese has melted. The eggs must be allowed to set softly.

4 As soon as the fonduta is velvety smooth and piping hot, serve it in warmed soup plates or shallow bowls with slices of toasted bread for dipping.

PER PORTION Energy 768kcal/3181kJ; Protein 36g; Carbohydrate 6g, of which sugars 3g; Fat 67g, of which saturates 40g; Cholesterol 356mg; Calcium 1162mg; Fibre 0.2g; Sodium 958mg.

PIEDMONTESE BAKED EGG AND CHEESE CUSTARD

TARTRA' PIEMONTESE

A rich and delicious, smooth eggy custard. This is the sort of dish to serve with lots of grissini, Piedmont's crisp and delicious breadsticks that are found in all the local bakeries. You could add chopped prosciutto or crumbled salame to this rich dish.

SERVES 4 TO 6

15g/½oz/1 tbsp unsalted butter, plus extra for greasing
flour, for dusting
1 onion, sliced
4 large eggs
2 egg yolks
500ml/17fl oz/2¼ cups full-fat (whole) milk
250ml/8fl oz/1 cup double (heavy) cream
45ml/3 tbsp freshly grated Parmesan cheese
30ml/2 tbsp mixed chopped fresh sage leaves and rosemary
a large pinch of grated nutmeg
sea salt and ground black pepper

1 Preheat the oven to 200°C/400°F/Gas 6. Grease and flour an ovenproof dish. Heat the butter in a frying pan over a low-medium heat, add the onion and fry until golden brown.

2 Beat the eggs and egg yolks together in a bowl with the milk, cream, Parmesan cheese, chopped herbs, nutmeg, and salt and pepper. Add the cooked onion and stir together.

3 Pour the mixture into the prepared ovenproof dish, then place the dish in a deep roasting pan. Pour water into the roasting pan to come halfway up the sides of the ovenproof dish.

4 Bake the custard for 30 minutes, or until the custard is set in the middle and crisp and golden on top.

PER PORTION Energy 355kcal/1468kJ; Protein 8g; Carbohydrate 6g, of which sugars 6g; Fat 33g, of which saturates 19g; Cholesterol 229mg; Calcium 194mg; Fibre 0.4g; Sodium 90mg.

PARMESAN AND TRUFFLE CANAPÉS
TARTINE AL PARMIGIANO REGGIANO

Piedmont is truly the land of truffles, and there are myriad recipes using them, such as these rich and filling little canapés. Truffles are a luxurious ingredient and can be very expensive, but this is a perfect recipe for an indulgent dinner party.

1 Cut 18 circles out of the slices of bread using a 7.5cm/3in round pastry (cookie) cutter and toast them all lightly.

2 Mix the Parmesan cheese with the softened butter and add the finely chopped truffle.

3 Spread or pipe this mixture on to the rounds of toast.

4 Just before you are ready to serve the canapés, garnish each one with a slice or two of truffle.

SERVES 6

9 slices white or brown bread
115g/4oz/1¼ cups freshly grated Parmesan cheese
115g/4oz/½ cup unsalted butter, softened
30g/1¼oz finely chopped truffle
a few slices of truffle, to garnish

PER PORTION Energy 314kcal/1433kJ; Protein 12g; Carbohydrate 24g, of which sugars 2g; Fat 23g, of which saturates 14g; Cholesterol 62mg; Calcium 274mg; Fibre 2g; Sodium 404mg.

SERVES 4

200g/7oz fresh soft goat's cheese
115g/4oz/1 1/4 cups freshly grated Parmesan cheese
75g/3oz/3/4 cup walnuts, finely chopped
65g/2 1/2oz/1 cup dried breadcrumbs
90ml/6 tbsp extra virgin olive oil
5ml/1 tsp mustard, such as savora or Dijon
200g/7oz mixed salad leaves
sea salt and ground black pepper

PER PORTION Energy 474kcal/1971kJ; Protein 26g; Carbohydrate 15g, of which sugars 3g; Fat 35g, of which saturates 16g; Cholesterol 73mg; Calcium 414mg; Fibre 1.5g; Sodium 659mg.

CHEESE AND WALNUT PATTIES
POLPETTINE DI FORMAGGIO CON LE NOCI

This is a traditional recipe from the province of Cuneo in Piedmont and is usually served as an antipasto. These little patties contain two types of cheese and the richness is perfectly offset by fresh salad leaves in a mustardy dressing.

1 Mix together the goat's cheese, Parmesan cheese and walnuts to form a thick paste.

2 Shape the paste into cherry-sized balls and flatten them slightly to make little patties. Coat the patties in the breadcrumbs.

3 Heat half the oil in a frying pan and fry the patties for 5 minutes, turning them over once or twice, until golden and crisp all over.

4 In a screw-top jar or dressing bottle, mix the remaining oil with the mustard and a little salt and pepper. Shake well.

5 Use the dressing to dress the salad leaves lightly, then arrange the leaves on four serving plates.

6 Place the hot cheese and walnut patties on top of the salad and serve immediately.

COURGETTE TART
TORTA DI ZUCCHETTI

This lovely courgette recipe comes from the Modena province in Emilia-Romagna. The pretty and versatile lattice-topped tart is cut into squares and can be served either warm or cold. It makes a perfect appetizer and it can form part of an antipasti selection, accompanied by other savoury tarts or antipasti dishes. It could also be served simply as a light lunch, with nothing but some crisp salad leaves on the side and a glass of refreshing white wine to wash it down.

1 Put the flour into a wide bowl and make a hollow in the centre with your fist. Add the ricotta cheese, the butter and a pinch of salt.

2 Rub the mixture together with your fingertips to make a soft ball of dough, adding a little water, if necessary. Cover and chill for 30 minutes, or until required.

3 To make the filling, cut the courgettes into 1cm/$^1/_2$in discs. Put them in a pan of lightly salted water, bring to the boil and simmer for about 5 minutes.

4 Drain the courgettes in a colander and return them to the same pan, but do not put it back on the heat. Add the butter to the pan and toss the courgettes in the butter until shiny, off the heat; the pan and courgettes should be warm enough to melt the butter.

5 Preheat the oven to 180°C/350°F/Gas 4. Grease and flour a 24cm/9$^1/_2$in flan tin (pan).

6 Mix the courgettes with the beaten eggs, mozzarella and Parmesan cheese, and season with salt and ground black pepper.

7 Roll out the pastry on a floured surface to a thickness of about 3mm/$^1/_8$in and use to line the flan tin, reserving about one-quarter of the pastry for the topping.

8 Pour the filling into the flan tin, spreading it out evenly with a fork.

9 Roll out the remaining pastry to a thickness of about 3mm/$^1/_8$in thick, then cut into 1cm/$^1/_2$in wide strips, long enough to cover the full length of the flan tin.

10 Arrange the strips in a lattice on top of the filling and brush with the beaten egg yolk.

11 Put the tart into the preheated oven and bake for 40–45 minutes, or until set and golden brown. Serve warm or cold, cut into squares.

SERVES 4

200g/7oz/1$^3/_4$ cups plain (all-purpose) flour
115g/4oz/$^1/_2$ cup ricotta cheese
115g/4oz/$^1/_2$ cup unsalted butter, softened and cubed
1 egg yolk, beaten
sea salt and ground black pepper
flour, for dusting
butter, for greasing

FOR THE FILLING

500g/1$^1/_4$lb courgettes (zucchini)
40g/1$^1/_2$oz/3 tbsp unsalted butter, softened
2 eggs, beaten
200g/7oz mozzarella cheese, cut into small dice
75g/3oz/1 cup freshly grated Parmesan cheese

PER PORTION Energy 790kcal/3308kJ; Protein 31g; Carbohydrate 42g, of which sugars 4g; Fat 57g, of which saturates 35g; Cholesterol 316mg; Calcium 573mg; Fibre 2.7g; Sodium 420mg.

COURGETTES WITH BREADCRUMBS
ZUCCHINE IN CARPIONE

A Lombard recipe which mimics the fish recipe of the same name. The phrase 'in Carpione' refers to food that is partially pickled by being cooked in vinegar, or at least has enough vinegar added to raise the level of acidity to the point when fermentation is naturally delayed. Many different kinds of food get treated in this way, not only in Lombardy, but in other areas of north-west Italy, and they reflect a time when refrigerators were not commonplace in every kitchen.

1 Trim and discard the ends from the courgettes, then cut them in half lengthways and remove the seeds using a spoon. Cut the courgettes into chunks.

2 Heat the oil in a pan and cook the onions gently for 5–10 minutes, or until softened.

3 Add the courgettes to the pan and cook them gently until completely soft.

4 Mix the breadcrumbs and vinegar together and stir this mixture through the courgettes and onions. Cook for a further 10 minutes, then serve hot, with toasted bread.

SERVES 4

600g/1lb 6oz courgettes (zucchini)
60ml/4 tbsp extra virgin olive oil
2 onions, finely sliced
75ml/5 tbsp soft white breadcrumbs
45ml/3 tbsp white wine vinegar
Italian bread, toasted, to serve

PER PORTION Energy 191kcal/788kJ; Protein 4g; Carbohydrate 9g, of which sugars 7g; Fat 16g, of which saturates 2g; Cholesterol 0mg; Calcium 57mg; Fibre 2.4g; Sodium 4mg.

SERVES 4 TO 6

6 large fennel bulbs (or 8 small ones)
185g/6½oz/generous ¾ cup unsalted butter, melted
185g/6½oz/generous 2 cups freshly grated Parmesan cheese, plus extra to serve
sea salt and ground black pepper

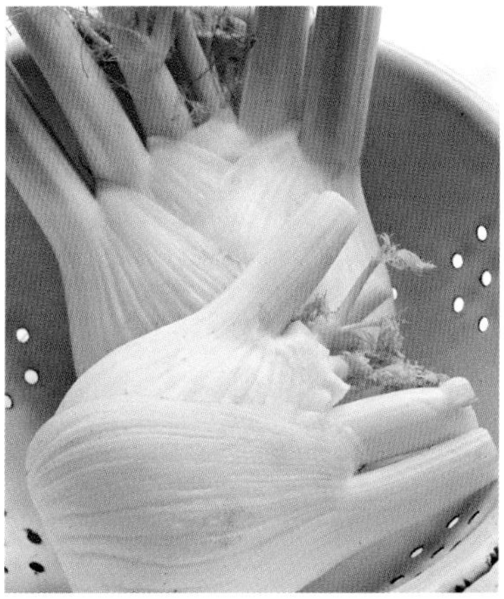

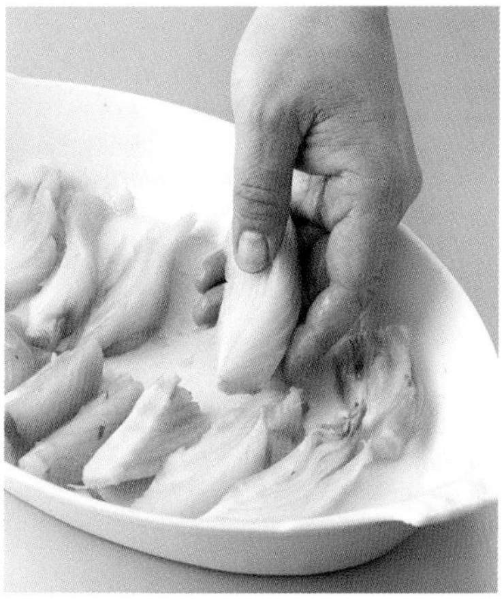

PER PORTION Energy 361kcal/1507kJ; Protein 12g; Carbohydrate 3g, of which sugars 2g; Fat 34g, of which saturates 22g; Cholesterol 96mg; Calcium 350mg; Fibre 3g; Sodium 250mg.

FENNEL WITH PARMESAN
FINOCCHI ALLA PARMIGIANA

Sliced fennel is layered with Parmesan cheese and drenched in butter in this dish from Emilia-Romagna. It's a lovely way to serve a very underrated vegetable and is particularly delicious served with fish or chicken.

1 Boil the whole fennel bulbs in salted water for 30 minutes, or until tender. Drain and cut them lengthways into finger-thick slices.

2 Preheat the oven to 180°C/350°F/Gas 4. Brush some of the melted butter over the base of an ovenproof dish.

3 Arrange half the fennel in a layer in the dish and cover with half the melted butter and Parmesan, then a sprinkling of salt and pepper. Repeat with the rest of the ingredients.

4 Bake for 20 minutes, or until golden, and serve, sprinkled with extra Parmesan.

SERVES 4

8 small, tender artichokes, trimmed
40g/1½oz/3 tbsp unsalted butter, melted
60ml/4 tbsp freshly grated Parmesan cheese, plus extra to serve

FOR THE SAUCE

50g/2oz/¼ cup unsalted butter
2 salted anchovies, boned and finely chopped
2 hard-boiled eggs, finely chopped
45ml/3 tbsp finely chopped fresh flat leaf parsley
sea salt

CAVOUR ARTICHOKES
CARCIOFI ALLA CAVOUR

This classic Piedmontese recipe for artichokes has lots of flavour, created from a rich sauce of anchovies and eggs. Serve it as an appetizer or as a side dish to accompany a simple meat dish or roast chicken.

1 Preheat the oven to 180°C/350°F/Gas 4. Boil the artichokes for 10–15 minutes in lightly salted water, until tender. Drain thoroughly.

2 Put the artichokes into an ovenproof dish. Cover with the melted butter and Parmesan, then transfer to the oven while you prepare the sauce, taking care that they do not burn.

3 To make the sauce, melt the butter in a small pan until just sizzling, then add the anchovies, eggs and parsley to the butter and stir together thoroughly. Cook for 3–4 minutes to heat through.

4 Pour the sauce over the artichokes and serve immediately, sprinkled with extra Parmesan.

PER PORTION Energy 264kcal/1106kJ; Protein 10g; Carbohydrate 2g, of which sugars 1g; Fat 25g, of which saturates 15g; Cholesterol 158mg; Calcium 162mg; Fibre 0.1g; Sodium 194mg.

SALSA VERDE

SALSA VERDE

Originating in Piedmont, this sauce now exists in many different variations. It adds a deliciously sharp tang to dishes like boiled meats or poached fish and is especially fabulous served with a classic bollito misto.

1 Wash and bone the anchovies. Chop the flat leaf parsley, garlic clove, anchovies and capers together very finely, then transfer to a mixing bowl.

2 Add the breadcrumbs, vinegar and tomato purée, and mix well together.

3 Remove the egg yolks from the halved hard-boiled eggs and chop them finely, then add to the anchovy mixture; discard the whites.

4 Stir gradually, adding enough olive oil to create a smooth textured, fairly thick sauce. Serve with simple fish or meat.

SERVES 6 TO 8

2 or 3 salted anchovies
50g/2oz fresh flat leaf parsley, leaves removed
1 garlic clove, peeled
15ml/1 tbsp salted capers
75ml/5 tbsp soft white breadcrumbs
30ml/2 tbsp white wine vinegar
5ml/1 tsp tomato purée (paste)
2 hard-boiled eggs, shelled and halved
60ml/4 tbsp extra virgin olive oil

PER PORTION Energy 125kcal/522kJ; Protein 3g; Carbohydrate 8g, of which sugars 1g; Fat 9g, of which saturates 1g; Cholesterol 49mg; Calcium 36mg; Fibre 0.6g; Sodium 138mg.

DESSERTS AND BAKING DOLCI

Dairy products including butter, eggs, cream and cheeses such as mascarpone and ricotta are used extensively in the desserts of north-west Italy, creating an extremely rich and luxurious feel to the sweet menu. Many recipes are tied closely to the land and its natural bounty, using ingredients like chestnuts, hazelnuts, almonds, walnuts and honey, while other recipes include local wines, dessert wines or Italian liqueurs to give a real depth of flavour. Chocolate is the pride of the city of Turin, and the Piedmont region is home to a fabulous array of chocolately desserts, with neighbouring Lombardy also having plenty to call its own. Fruits, especially orchard fruits, are used in many desserts, often being steeped in red wine, baked until gooey and sweet, or added to a cake.

MASCARPONE, CREAM AND PIEDMONTESE CHOCOLATE

In no other region in Italy has the difference from one city to another, from one area to another, been so marked as in Lombardy; perhaps it is the dense winter fogs and the deep snow that has always isolated one community from another across the wide plains and in the high mountains. This region is home to some of the most noble cheeses in the country, including ricotta and mascarpone, both of which are used in the preparation of many desserts. Butter, too, is produced and used as a principal ingredient in Lombard cooking, especially in cake- and pastry-making.

Piedmont owes much of its dessert-making skills and culinary expertise to its link with France, most obvious in the creation of the fabulous Zabaglione, a very close cousin of the French sabayon. Chocolate is much-loved in Piedmont and appears in a multitude of recipes. Of all the chocolate made in Piedmont, the world-famous Giandujotto deserves a special mention. This little chocolate, which with its long triangular shape looks a little like an upturned boat, is made from a mixture of cocoa butter, sugar and Piedmont's celebrated round hazelnuts, which are admired throughout the country for their quality and taste.

Turin became the chocolate capital of Italy during the waves of migration of the Protestant community between the 18th and 19th centuries. When families returned from their exile in France or Switzerland, they brought with them the secrets of the celebrated chefs and the skills of the chocolatiers from the other side of the Alps. The famous Piedmontese chocolate industry grew out of the experience of those pioneers and is still very much alive today.

PEARS POACHED IN RED WINE

PERE COTTE NEL VINO ROSSO

In Piedmont and the Aosta Valley they'll tell you that the best possible pear for making this essentially simple dessert is the highly sought-after martin sec variety. While this may be a difficult fruit to find outside of the area, what is most essential is that the pears you use must be sweet and full of flavour, yet firm enough to keep their shape as they poach. Use the best possible red wine you can afford for maximum taste. Serve with cream, ice cream or mascarpone, if you like.

SERVES 6

- 6 firm pears, peeled, left whole with stalks on
- ½ cinnamon stick
- 75ml/5 tbsp caster (superfine) sugar
- 750ml/1¼ pints/3 cups red wine
- cream, ice cream or mascarpone, to serve (optional)

1 Cut a slice from the base of each pear so that they will stand up firmly.

2 Stand all the pears upright in a pan. Add the cinnamon and the sugar.

3 Pour over the wine and bring to the boil, then reduce the heat to low and cover with a lid.

4 Simmer very slowly until the pears are soft, turning them frequently so that they become completely soaked and coloured by the wine.

5 Transfer to a bowl and cool, turning frequently. Discard the cinnamon stick. If you like, you can serve the pears standing upright on serving plates, accompanied by cream, ice cream or plain mascarpone.

COOK'S TIP

- The longer you leave the pears in the wine, the darker they will become.
- You may like to reduce the wine to a syrup, and then drizzle it over the pears before serving.

PER PORTION Energy 196kcal/826kJ; Protein 1g; Carbohydrate 29g, of which sugars 29g; Fat 0g, of which saturates 0g; Cholesterol 0mg; Calcium 27mg; Fibre 2.6g; Sodium 14mg.

BAKED PEACHES
PESCHE AL FORNO

This simple peach dessert can be made with nectarines, though it is especially good with the last of the season's peaches, which are slightly more woolly and therefore able to absorb the wine and the other flavours much more easily.

1 Preheat the oven to 190°C/375°F/Gas 5 and grease an ovenproof dish.

2 Cut the peaches in half. Remove and discard the stones (pits). Scoop out about half of the flesh and transfer to a bowl.

3 Mash the removed flesh with the crumbled amaretti, the butter, sugar and almonds. Moisten the mixture with a little of the Marsala, just enough to make a sticky texture.

4 Fill all the peaches evenly with the mixture.

5 Arrange the peaches in the prepared dish and surround with the remaining wine. Cover loosely with foil and bake, basting occasionally, for 30 minutes, or until the peaches are tender.

6 Remove the foil and place a square of chocolate on top of each peach half. Increase the temperature of the oven to 220°C/425°F/ Gas 7 and bake the peaches for 5–10 minutes until the tops are lightly crisp and the chocolate has just melted. Alternatively, slide them under a hot grill (broiler) for about 5 minutes. Serve hot or cold.

SERVES 6

- 15g/½oz/1 tbsp unsalted butter, softened, plus extra for greasing
- 6 large peaches
- 6 amaretti, crumbled finely
- 50g/2oz/¼ cup caster (superfine) sugar
- 25g/1oz/¼ cup blanched almonds, chopped
- 150ml/¼ pint/⅔ cup Marsala
- 12 squares cooking chocolate (unsweetened)

PER PORTION Energy 217kcal/913kJ; Protein 4g; Carbohydrate 30g, of which sugars 28g; Fat 8g, of which saturates 3g; Cholesterol 6mg; Calcium 28mg; Fibre 2.9g; Sodium 7mg.

ZABAGLIONE
ZABAGLIONE

This is a true labour of love, a combination of fresh egg yolks, Marsala wine and sugar, beaten into a frothy mousse texture that is just warm. It is a very light dessert, delicious with poached apples, amaretti, savoiardi biscuits or slices of Panettone.

1 Mix the egg yolks, wine and caster sugar together in a large, round, heatproof bowl.

2 Place the bowl over a pan of very hot, but not boiling, water.

3 Whisk for 20 minutes (or 10 minutes with an electric whisk), or until foaming, thick and shiny.

4 Pour the mixture into stemmed wine glasses and serve with amaretti, if you like.

SERVES 4

4 egg yolks
60ml/4 tbsp dessert wine, Marsala or sweet sherry
60ml/4 tbsp caster (superfine) sugar
amaretti, to serve (optional)

PER PORTION Energy 134kcal/563kJ; Protein 3g; Carbohydrate 17g, of which sugars 17g; Fat 5g, of which saturates 2g; Cholesterol 202mg; Calcium 27mg; Fibre 0g; Sodium 12mg.

SERVES 8

65g/2½oz/5 tbsp butter, cut into small pieces, plus extra for greasing
45ml/3 tbsp stale breadcrumbs
3 large (US extra large) eggs
150g/5oz/¾ cup caster (superfine) sugar, plus extra for dusting
200g/7oz/1¾ cups plain (all-purpose) flour
150ml/¼ pint/⅔ cup milk
grated rind of ½ lemon
7.5ml/1½ tsp baking powder
1kg/2¼lb eating apples, peeled and thinly sliced
175g/6oz/1 cup blackberries
30ml/2 tbsp light brown sugar

PER PORTION Energy 415kcal/1756kJ; Protein 8g; Carbohydrate 79g, of which sugars 56g; Fat 10g, of which saturates 5g; Cholesterol 114mg; Calcium 118mg; Fibre 3.6g; Sodium 235mg.

ITALIAN APPLE CAKE
TORTA DI MELE

This is the simplest and most delicious of apple cakes. Make sure you use sweet and tasty eating apples rather than cooking apples. When in season, peaches, apricots, nectarines and plums all work well too.

1 Preheat the oven to 180°C/350°F/Gas 4. Grease a 25cm/10in cake tin (pan) with butter, then dust with the breadcrumbs.

2 Beat the eggs in a large mixing bowl. Add the sugar gradually, beating until light and fluffy.

3 Fold in the flour, milk, lemon rind and baking powder. The mixture should be quite liquid.

4 Turn the tin upside down to remove all the loose breadcrumbs. Discard them.

5 Add half the sliced apples and half the blackberries to the cake mixture (batter) and stir through.

6 Pour the cake mixture into the tin and arrange the remaining sliced apples and blackberries on top. Dot with butter, sprinkle with the light brown sugar and bake for 55 minutes.

7 Take the cake out of the oven and cool completely, then remove from the tin. Serve sprinkled with extra caster sugar.

PIEDMONTESE CHOCOLATE PUDDING

BUNET

Chocolate, amaretti and coffee make a marvellous combination of flavours in this luxurious chilled pudding. It is very rich, so doesn't really need anything else to go with it, although you can serve it with very cold single cream for extra decadence.

1 Preheat the oven to 160°C/325°F/Gas 3. Put the milk and the amaretti in a pan, bring to the boil, then immediately remove from the heat.

2 Break up the amaretti completely with a spoon. Stir in the drinking chocolate powder.

3 In a large mixing bowl, beat the eggs and caster sugar together until pale and fluffy, then pour this mixture into the pan containing the milk and amaretti. Stir carefully to fold in and amalgamate everything together, then stir in the coffee.

4 Put the granulated sugar and 30ml/2 tbsp cold water into a small pan and heat together until the sugar has caramelized. Coat the base of a loaf tin (pan) or a mould with the caramel.

5 Pour the mixture into the tin or mould and place it in a roasting pan. Pour enough water around the tin or mould to come halfway up the side.

6 Place the roasting pan in the oven and bake for 30–40 minutes, or until a knife inserted into the centre comes out clean.

7 Remove from the oven, allow to cool, then chill slightly before turning out of the tin or mould and cutting into eight slices. Serve drizzled with single cream, if you like.

SERVES 8

1 litre/1¾ pints/4 cups milk
250g/9oz amaretti
15ml/1 tbsp drinking chocolate powder
6 large (US extra large) eggs, beaten
150g/5oz/¾ cup caster (superfine) sugar
1 espresso (about 30ml/2 tbsp very strong black coffee)
90ml/6 tbsp granulated (white) sugar
single (light) cream, to serve (optional)

COOK'S TIPS

- When baked in a loaf tin (pan), the pudding can be sliced into neat sections very easily.
- You can also use eight individual moulds. The cooking time will have to be reduced to 20 minutes.

PER PORTION Energy 409kcal/1712kJ; Protein 16g; Carbohydrate 55g, of which sugars 44g; Fat 15g, of which saturates 4g; Cholesterol 198mg; Calcium 184mg; Fibre 0.7g; Sodium 131mg.

ITALIAN CHOCOLATE CAKE
TORTA AL CIOCCOLATO

Experienced cake makers will notice that the method for making this cake from Lombardy is quite unusual. Here, all the ingredients are added to beaten egg whites, not the other way around, which gives it quite a distinct texture.

1 Preheat the oven to 180°C/350°F/Gas 4. Grease and line a 23cm/9in loose-based cake tin (pan) with baking parchment.

2 Melt the chocolate in a heatproof bowl over a pan of gently simmering water.

3 While the chocolate is melting, put the egg whites into a clean, grease-free bowl and whisk until they form stiff peaks.

4 Remove the melted chocolate from the pan and stir in the butter, then add the coffee.

5 Carefully fold the sugar into the egg whites.

6 Mix the baking powder with the cocoa powder and flour in a bowl.

7 Stir the egg yolks into the melted chocolate, then gently fold this mixture into the egg whites.

8 Sift over the flour and cocoa mixture and gently fold in with a large metal spoon. Turn into the prepared tin.

9 Bake for 40 minutes, or until a skewer inserted into the centre comes out clean.

10 Leave to cool in the cake tin, then turn out and cover with melted chocolate.

SERVES 6 TO 8

- 130g/4½oz/generous ½ cup unsalted butter, cubed, plus extra for greasing
- 250g/9oz dark (bittersweet) chocolate, chopped
- 5 large (US extra large) eggs, separated
- 1 espresso (about 30ml/2 tbsp very strong black coffee)
- 200g/7oz/1 cup caster (superfine) sugar
- 5ml/1 tsp baking powder
- 30ml/2 tbsp unsweetened cocoa powder
- 115g/4oz/1 cup plain (all-purpose) flour
- 400g/14oz chocolate, melted, to cover

PER PORTION Energy 757kcal/3181kJ; Protein 12g; Carbohydrate 90g, of which sugars 77g; Fat 42g, of which saturates 24g; Cholesterol 201mg; Calcium 87mg; Fibre 2.9g; Sodium 162mg.

SERVES 6 TO 8

200g/7oz/scant 1 cup unsalted butter, melted, plus extra for greasing
150g/5oz/1¼ cups plain (all-purpose) flour, plus extra for dusting
6 eggs, separated
90ml/6 tbsp caster (superfine) sugar
50g/2oz/½ cup cornflour (cornstarch)
5ml/1 tsp baking powder
7.5ml/1½ tsp grated lemon rind
pinch of salt
icing (confectioners') sugar, for dusting

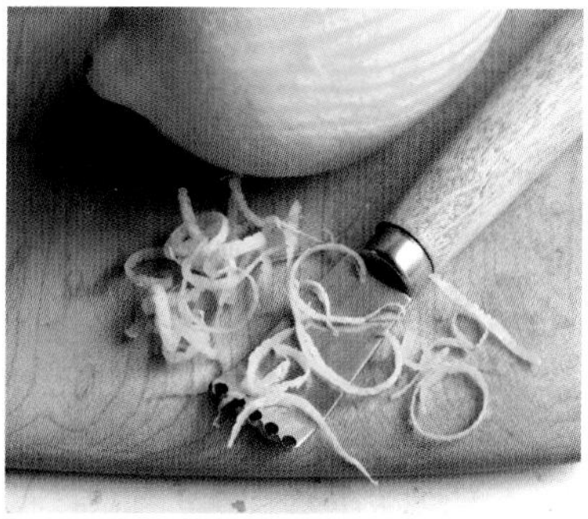

PER PORTION Energy 386kcal/1620kJ; Protein 8g; Carbohydrate 32g, of which sugars 12g; Fat 26g, of which saturates 15g; Cholesterol 231mg; Calcium 65mg; Fibre 0.6g; Sodium 130mg.

DAISY CAKE
LA TORTA MARGHERITA

This classic cake is traditionally served at tea time for merenda (the snack that children have after their siesta). It is a plain sponge cake, usually covered with a thick layer of icing sugar, or split in half with a chocolate or jam filling. It tends to be rather dry, and is enjoyed dunked into a bowl of milk, hot chocolate or coffee, or a little dessert wine for adults. It is delightful by itself, and it is also an excellent base for making an Italian trifle, or any other Italian pudding that requires a plain cake base.

1 Preheat the oven to 180°C/350°F/Gas 4. Grease and flour a 25cm/10in cake tin (pan).

2 In a large bowl, beat the egg yolks with the sugar until pale yellow.

3 Sift the flour, cornflour and baking powder into a separate bowl, then gradually beat these dry ingredients into the egg mixture.

4 Gradually beat in the melted butter, lemon rind and salt.

5 Put the egg whites into a clean, grease-free bowl and whisk until they form stiff peaks. Fold into the cake mixture (batter).

6 Pour the cake mixture into the cake tin and bake for 40 minutes, or until a clean knife inserted into the centre comes out clean.

7 Cool in the cake tin for 15 minutes, then turn out on to a wire rack to finish cooling. Dust with a thick layer of icing sugar just before serving.

PANNA COTTA
PANNA COTTA

This delicious Piedmontese speciality is gaining in popularity all over Italy and throughout the world. You can make it completely plain, if you like, or add flavourings such as crushed amaretti, coffee, chocolate, soft fruits, citrus rind or liqueur – the possibilities are endless. The skill of making this dessert lies in getting it to set without being rubbery, so just the right amount of sheet gelatine needs to be used. Trial and error will help you find out what works best for you.

SERVES 8

1 litre/$1^3/_4$ pints/4 cups single (light) cream
50g/2oz/$^1/_2$ cup icing (confectioners') sugar
3 or 4 sheets gelatine
60ml/4 tbsp granulated or caster (superfine) sugar

1 Divide the single cream in half and put it into two separate pans. Bring the cream in both pans to just under the boil over a low-medium heat. To one pan of cream add the icing sugar, and to the other add the sheets of gelatine.

2 Whisk the cream in both pans constantly until the sugar and gelatine have completely dissolved and the cream is very hot but not boiling. It might be a good idea to get someone to help you do the whisking, or you can whisk with both hands, if you can manage it.

3 Pour the cream from both pans into one bowl and whisk together. Allow the mixture to cool completely.

4 While the mixture is cooling, put the sugar into a small pan and melt over a low heat without stirring until caramelized to a light blond colour.

5 Coat the base of eight small metal moulds or ramekins with the caramel. (Alternatively, divide the sugar between the moulds and melt it over a low flame to lightly caramelize.) Allow the caramel in the ramekins to cool.

6 Strain the cooled panna cotta into the moulds and put into the refrigerator to set until required. When firmly set, dip the moulds into boiling water for 5 seconds and turn out on to cold plates.

COOK'S TIP

If you want to add a flavouring, do so at step 3, once you have whisked the two cream mixtures together. Try the grated rind of 1 lemon, 1 espresso (30ml/2 tbsp strong black coffee), 45ml/3 tbsp liqueur or brandy, or 10ml/2 tsp vanilla extract. Decorate before serving with grated lemon rind, fruit coulis or ground coffee beans.

PER PORTION Energy 302kcal/1255kJ; Protein 4g; Carbohydrate 18g, of which sugars 18g; Fat 24g, of which saturates 15g; Cholesterol 69mg; Calcium 113mg; Fibre 0g; Sodium 39mg.

CHESTNUT, CREAM AND CHOCOLATE MOUNTAIN
IL MONTEBIANCO

A potato ricer, mouli or food mill will be required for this classic, luxurious Piedmontese recipe, which is a perfect dinner-party finale.

SERVES 10 TO 12

- 300g/11oz/generous 1½ cups caster (superfine) sugar
- 1kg/2¼lb/9 cups fresh chestnuts, marrons if possible, peeled (see Cook's Tip) or 675g/1½lb/6 cups peeled chestnuts
- pinch of salt
- 60ml/4 tbsp Strega liqueur (optional)
- 750ml/1¼ pints/3 cups double (heavy) or whipping cream
- 75ml/5 tbsp sifted icing (confectioners') sugar
- 5ml/1 tsp vanilla extract
- 6 large ready-made meringues, crushed
- 150g/5oz good-quality dark (bittersweet) chocolate, with minimum 60 per cent cocoa solids
- 30ml/2 tbsp good-quality drinking chocolate powder
- 6 glacé marrons and 12 candied violets, to decorate

COOK'S TIP

To peel fresh chestnuts, preheat the oven to 200°C/400°F/Gas 6, then cut a cross-shaped slit into each one. Lay them on a baking sheet and cook for 15 minutes, or until the skins begin to curl where they have been cut. Peel them while still hot, holding them in a dish towel, then set them aside.

1 Put 120ml/4fl oz/½ cup cold water into a pan and add the sugar. Heat slowly until a syrup is formed at the thread stage (this is 107°C/225°F if you have a sugar thermometer; or when placed in cold water the syrup forms a fine, soft thread).

2 Add the peeled chestnuts to the syrup with a pinch of salt, and poach very gently for about 30 minutes.

3 Add the Strega, if using. Remove the chestnuts from the syrup using a slotted spoon and set aside. Reduce the syrup by about one-third over a medium heat, then add the chestnuts again. Set aside to cool.

4 Put the cream into a bowl with the icing sugar and the vanilla extract, and whip it until it forms stiff peaks. Divide the cream evenly into three separate bowls.

5 Mix three of the crushed meringues into one bowl of whipped cream. Divide the chocolate in half and melt one half in a heatproof bowl over a pan of gently simmering water. Mix the melted chocolate into the second bowl of whipped cream. Leave the third bowl plain. Chill all three bowls of cream until required.

6 Melt the remaining chocolate in a heatproof bowl over a pan of gently simmering water.

7 Push the chestnuts and reduced syrup through a ricer or a food mill so that they fall in strands into the bottom of your serving bowls, reserving some for the top.

8 Cover the chesnut strands with a layer of chocolate cream, then a layer of meringue cream, then finally the plain cream. None of these layers need to be smooth and even, they can all overlap and be as uneven as you like.

9 Crumble the remaining meringue on the top of the mound to symbolize the white peak, so that you can see still plenty of the plain white cream around it.

10 Decorate the slopes of your Montebianco with the remaining chestnut strands. Drizzle with the melted chocolate and dust with a little drinking chocolate powder. Chill and serve within 8 hours.

11 Just before serving, arrange the glacé marrons and candied violets on top for decoration.

PER PORTION Energy 671kcal/2804kJ; Protein 4g; Carbohydrate 80g, of which sugars 55g; Fat 39g, of which saturates 23g; Cholesterol 86mg; Calcium 79mg; Fibre 3.8g; Sodium 40mg.

INDEX

PUBLISHER'S ACKNOWLEDGEMENTS
The publisher would like to thank the following for permission to reproduce their images: 7tl Danny Lehman/Corbis; 7tr Robert Everts/Corbis; 9t and 9br Stephanie Maze/Corbis; 9bl Hulton-Deutsch Collection/Corbis; 10l imagebroker/Alamy; 11tl Vittoriano Rastelli/Corbis; 11tr, 12tl and 14 Owen Franken/Corbis; 12tr Paul Almasy/Corbis; 13bl and 13br CuboImages srl/Alamy; 15tl Gio Spazz/Alamy; 15tr Atlantide Phototravel/Corbis; 8, 37, 46, 52, 58, 68, 84, 93, 98, 104, 118, 122, 125 iStockphoto.